MASTERING SINGLE-FAMILY REAL ESTATE

A BEGINNER'S GUIDE TO PROFITABLE INVESTMENTS

JAMES SANTIAGO

DEDICATION

*To my three amazing children—Caia, Stephen, and Mica—who fill my life
with love and purpose: you are my everything.
This book is for all the dreamers and go-getters across the world who are
tired of trading their time for money and long for the freedom to create
income while they sleep. May this guide help you break free, build wealth,
and unlock a life of purpose and possibility.
You've inspired me to share this journey, and I hope it becomes a catalyst for
yours.*

DISCLAIMER

This book is for **educational purposes only**. Real estate laws, tax regulations, and market conditions vary by location and individual circumstances.

Always consult with:
- A **licensed real estate professional**
- A **certified tax advisor or CPA**
- Or a **legal professional**

...before making any investment decisions.

While every effort has been made to ensure accuracy, this book does **not guarantee financial results**, nor does it replace personalized advice.

For full terms and disclaimers, visit:
   LearnWealthy.us/disclaimer

ROADMAP TO SUCCESS (TABLE OF CONTENTS)

PREFACE

Real estate has transformed my life in ways I never could have imagined. As both a real estate agent and investor, I've seen firsthand how this industry can unlock financial freedom and provide a foundation for lasting wealth. My journey began with a simple goal: to create income while I sleep and break free from the cycle of trading time for money. What I didn't expect was how much I would enjoy sharing what I've learned.

Through my YouTube channel, Learn Wealthy, I've discovered my love for teaching. It's a platform by which I help others navigate the world of real estate, investing, finance, and economics—topics that are not just professional pursuits but personal passions. Teaching has deepened my commitment to empowering people to change their lives and build wealth on their own terms.

This book is a culmination of years of experience, lessons learned, and the desire to provide a practical, accessible guide to mastering single-family real estate. It's written for anyone ready to take their first step into real estate or those looking to scale their portfolio. I aim to demystify the process and show that success in this field is achievable for anyone willing to learn and take action.

My journey as an author has only just begun. This book will be the first of many as I continue to explore and share insights about real estate, investing, and the broader world of finance and economics. I hope these pages inspire you, equip you with the tools you need, and spark the same passion for real estate that drives me every day.

Thank you for allowing me to be part of your journey. Let's build wealth together.

James Santiago

Real Estate Investor, Agent, and Founder of the Learn Wealthy YouTube channel

INTRODUCTION: CHARTING YOUR PATH TO REAL ESTATE SUCCESS

Welcome to *Mastering Single-Family Real Estate: A Beginner's Guide to Profitable Investments.*

If you've ever dreamed of building wealth, creating financial freedom, and securing a better future, you're holding the right guide in your hands. This book is not just a collection of strategies and insights, but it is also a road map designed to transform your life through the power of real estate investing.

The Opportunity Awaits

For decades, real estate has been one of the most reliable paths to wealth. Unlike stocks or cryptocurrencies, it offers the stability of a tangible asset while providing income and appreciation over time. And among the various types of real estate investments, single-family homes stand out as an accessible and low-risk entry point for beginners.

But let's be honest: embarking on this journey can feel intimidating. Questions swirl.

- Where do I start?
- How do I know if a property is a good deal?
- Can I do this without a lot of money?

This book answers those questions and many more. Whether you're taking your first steps into real estate or looking to scale a budding portfolio, the tools and knowledge shared here will equip you to make informed decisions, avoid common pitfalls, and achieve your investment goals.

Why Real Estate? Why Now?

Real estate isn't just about property. It's about people, opportunity, and long-term security. Unlike other investments, real estate gives you control. You can influence its value through improvements, adjust your strategy based on market trends, and build equity while other people—your tenants—pay down your mortgage.

The market is always evolving, but one truth remains constant: people will always need places to live. This enduring demand makes single-family homes a resilient and rewarding investment option. Now is the time to leverage this opportunity—to turn your aspirations into action.

What You'll Learn

This book guides you through every stage of the real estate journey:

- Understanding the Foundations: Learn what makes real estate a unique and powerful wealth-building tool.
- The Economics of Success: Gain insight into market trends, supply and demand, and how external factors affect your investments.
- Applying Practical Strategies: Learn actionable steps to navigate each phase of the process, from financing options to property management.

- Scaling Your Portfolio: Explore advanced strategies for expanding your holdings and maximizing returns.

Each chapter contains real-world examples, actionable advice, and insights drawn from years of experience. You'll also find personal stories—my triumphs and lessons learned—to inspire and reassure you that success is within reach.

My Promise to You

This isn't a get-rich-quick manual or a generic self-help book. It's a practical, down-to-earth guide for anyone willing to put in the work to achieve their financial dreams. My promise is simple: If you commit to learning and applying what's in these pages, you'll gain the confidence and tools needed to make real estate a cornerstone of your financial future.

Let's Get Started

Real estate changed my life, and I believe it can change yours too. This journey is about more than money; it's about freedom, purpose, and leaving a legacy. So take a deep breath, turn the page, and let's build the future you've always envisioned. Together we'll unlock the doors to opportunity—one property at a time.

CHAPTER 1: UNDERSTANDING REAL ESTATE: MORE THAN JUST PROPERTY

When most people think of real estate, they picture houses, apartments, or sprawling office buildings. But real estate is so much more than just property—it's a foundational pillar of our economy, a tangible asset that holds value through changing times, and one of the most accessible paths to building long-term wealth.

What Is Real Estate?

Real estate encompasses land and everything permanently attached to it, whether naturally occurring or man-made. This includes homes, office buildings, factories, and even undeveloped land waiting for its next purpose. Broadly speaking, real estate falls into four major categories:

1. **Residential properties**, such as single-family homes, apartments, and condominiums, which are designed for living and are the most familiar form of real estate.
2. **Commercial properties** serve business purposes, ranging

from office spaces to retail stores and bustling shopping centers.

3. **Industrial real estate** is geared toward manufacturing, production, and storage, including warehouses and factories that drive large-scale operations.

4. **Land** represents raw, undeveloped property, including agricultural land and parcels earmarked for future development.

Each category offers its own investment opportunities. But residential real estate—especially single-family homes—stands out as the most accessible and popular choice for investors building long-term wealth.

Why Single-Family Real Estate?

For those just beginning their journey into real estate, single-family homes present the most accessible, stable, and low-risk investment opportunity. Let's break down why single-family homes are a smart choice for new investors.

Low Risk—Stability in a changing market: Single-family homes are one of the most stable and reliable real estate investments, especially when compared to commercial or industrial properties. Housing demand remains constant because everyone needs a place to live—making single-family homes far less vulnerable to market downturns. While other sectors, such as office buildings or shopping malls, can face sharp price fluctuations during economic shifts, single-family homes typically hold steady, offering more resilience.

The value of single-family homes is largely driven by the sale prices of comparable properties in the area, not by the income the property generates. This makes single-family homes less susceptible to drastic changes. In contrast, commercial real estate or large multi-family properties rely heavily on the income they generate, which can fluctuate based on tenant demand and economic conditions.

Often, even during economic downturns, single-family homes

retain or steadily increase in value over time. By maintaining the property well, you can rest assured that it will hold or increase in value, making it a solid investment for those seeking stability and long-term growth.

A Valuable Educational Experience: Investing in a single-family home is like enrolling in a real-world real estate masterclass—except instead of sitting in a classroom, you're building wealth while you learn. Unlike larger, more complex investments, a single-family property is manageable, scalable, and a perfect starting point for new investors looking to gain hands-on experience.

From financing the deal to managing tenants and handling repairs, you'll quickly develop the skills needed to navigate the real estate landscape. You'll learn how to fund a property using traditional mortgages or creative financing strategies, getting a firsthand look at what it takes to secure capital and structure deals. Managing the property teaches you the ins and outs of tenant relations, maintenance, and repairs, giving you a taste of what it means to run a rental business. And as you analyze market trends, assess property values, and pinpoint profitable locations, you'll sharpen your ability to identify great deals before others do.

Beyond real estate itself, single-family investing teaches valuable business fundamentals. You'll gain experience in bookkeeping, networking with industry professionals, and learning how tax deductions can maximize your profits. You'll also build relationships with contractors, mortgage brokers, and real estate agents, setting the stage for future deals and a growing portfolio.

For anyone serious about building long-term wealth through real estate, starting with a single-family home is the smartest first move. It's an opportunity to earn while you learn, refine your investment strategy, and lay the foundation for a successful real estate career.

Accessibility—Easier to Finance and Less Capital-Intensive: For first-time investors, single-family homes are typically more affordable than multifamily or commercial properties. They require less capital up front and are easier to finance.

In this book, you'll learn about various financing options, such as conventional loans, FHA loans, and other funding strategies tailored for first-time buyers. These loans often come with lower down-payment requirements and simpler approval processes, making single-family homes a more accessible option for many investors. Compared with commercial or multifamily properties, which often require larger down payments and more complex financing structures, single-family homes provide a smoother path into real estate investment.

Scalability—Building Wealth over Time: One of the most powerful benefits of real estate is its scalability. Starting with a single-family home creates a foundation on which you can scale your investments as you gain more experience and confidence.

Scalability is critical for growing any business or personal wealth. Without it, your income is tied directly to the time you invest. And as we know, time is more valuable than money; once it's gone, it's gone forever. This is the limitation of traditional jobs: your income is capped by the number of hours you work. In contrast, real estate investing allows you to build income streams that don't depend directly on your time. As you scale, you can generate more income without putting in more hours.

By starting small with a single-family home, you can gradually expand your portfolio—acquiring multifamily properties or commercial real estate, or branching into other types of investments. The ability to scale your income through real estate allows you to break free from the limitations of time-for-money exchanges, opening doors to greater financial freedom.

Real Estate—A Tangible Asset and Economic Driver: One of the most significant advantages of real estate is its tangibility. Unlike stocks, bonds, or cryptocurrencies, you can see, touch, and physically interact with real estate. This physical presence provides security—especially during market crashes. While values may fluctuate, real estate has inherent value as shelter, which tends to hold through economic instability.

Real estate also drives the economy in profound ways. Housing construction and sales contribute billions to the economy each year. Beyond that, real estate creates millions of jobs across industries—from builders and contractors to real estate agents and financiers. Real estate is not just an investment—it's a cornerstone of economic stability and growth.

Real Estate's Role in Building Wealth: Real estate is one of the most effective ways to build long-term wealth, both on a personal and a national level. Owning property often represents an individual's most valuable asset. Over time, single-family homes appreciate in value, allowing you to build wealth through equity. As the property appreciates and you pay down your mortgage, your ownership stake in the home grows, increasing your net worth.

On a larger scale, real estate is a vital economic engine. Governments rely on property taxes, and stable housing markets help drive national economies. Simply put, real estate is not just about buying property—it's about securing a valuable asset that can grow in value and provide income.

My Journey into Real Estate

Let me share a bit about my own journey into real estate. Like many of you, my interest in real estate started early. I was in high school in the Philippines when I first read *Rich Dad Poor Dad* by Robert Kiyosaki in 2003. The book planted the seed in me that would eventually grow into a deep passion for real estate investing. Back then, I didn't fully understand the concepts of bonds or real estate that Kiyosaki was talking about, but the core idea that being an entrepreneur was the way to financial freedom stuck with me. I came from a modest background—neither of my parents were rich, and they couldn't teach me anything about investing or financial independence.

In 2006, I moved to Santa Clarita, California, to attend college. I pursued a nursing degree, but Kiyosaki's words were still with me. While I was pursuing my nursing degree, I also started taking business courses at my local community college—classes such as Accounting 101, Economics, and Business Law—alongside my nursing prerequisites. I read more books, attended seminars, and even got swept up in those "get-rich-quick" real estate seminars.

It wasn't until 2015 that I truly got my feet wet in the world of real estate. I became a licensed real estate agent in California and started working in real estate transactions. The firsthand experience of working with clients, understanding contracts, and negotiating deals provided me with an invaluable understanding of how real estate works.

Looking back, I now see how much that early exposure to real estate and my relentless pursuit of knowledge shaped my journey. I still remember the first time I closed on a rental property—signing the papers, holding the keys, and realizing that I had just taken my first real step toward financial freedom. It wasn't all smooth sailing. I made mistakes, underestimated repair costs, and dealt with difficult tenants. But each challenge taught me invaluable lessons. Whether from books, seminars, or hands-on experience, these lessons have given me the confidence to keep growing my real estate portfolio and teaching others to do the same. I've learned firsthand the power of real estate as a tool for financial freedom, and it has become a cornerstone of my wealth-building strategy.

Key Takeaways

As we've explored in this chapter, real estate is far more than just a collection of properties—it's a tangible asset that stands the test of time, it is a key driver of economic growth, and it is a powerful vehicle for wealth-building. While various types of real estate investments offer unique opportunities, single-family homes stand out as the ideal entry point for new investors.

Investing in single-family homes provides a low-risk, stable foundation from which you can gain valuable hands-on experience in real estate. As you learn the ropes and build your portfolio, you'll have the opportunity to scale up, increasing your wealth without being tied to the limitations of traditional work. Real estate offers scalable income streams that grow independently of the time you put in, helping you break free from the traditional 9-to-5 grind.

In the chapters ahead, we'll dive deeper into the mechanics of real estate investing, explore financing options, and look at the tools you need to start building your own wealth through real estate.

CHAPTER 2: THE EVOLUTION OF REAL ESTATE

Real Estate: Yesterday, Today, and Forever

Real estate cannot be lost or stolen, nor can it be carried away. Purchased with common sense, paid for in full, and managed with reasonable care, it is about the safest investment in the world.

— FRANKLIN D. ROOSEVELT

Picture this: thousands of years ago in ancient Mesopotamia, a merchant acquires a plot of fertile land. To the untrained eye, it's just soil. But to the merchant, it's the key to a future of prosperity. That land will feed his family, sustain trade, and establish his household as a cornerstone of the community.

Fast forward to today. The fields of Mesopotamia are long gone, replaced by sprawling suburban neighborhoods, towering skyscrapers, and bustling urban centers. Yet the fundamental truth hasn't changed. Owning real estate still secures wealth, builds stability, and shapes legacies. From single-family homes to cutting-edge commercial properties, real estate remains one of the most reliable tools for creating a better future.

Why is that? Why does real estate endure as a cornerstone of wealth? It's simple: land meets an eternal, unchanging human need. People will always need a place to live, work, and gather. While markets rise and fall, technologies disrupt industries, and currencies even collapse, the demand for land and shelter persists.

Think about it: real estate isn't just property—it's security, influence, and freedom. People have fought wars over it, built empires on it, and secured fortunes through it. Whether in ancient Mesopotamia or today's housing market, the story remains the same—owning real estate gives you control over a resource that everyone values.

A Timeless Wealth-Building Strategy

Buy land; they're not making it anymore.

— MARK TWAIN

Real estate isn't tied to fleeting trends or fads. It's rooted in fundamental human needs. Throughout history, monarchs, merchants, and modern investors have used property to build not just their wealth but also their influence.

Take my own journey, for example. As someone passionate about real estate, I've seen firsthand how its role evolves with society. Today, I'm actively learning and adapting to new technologies such as blockchain, virtual reality tours, and smart property-management tools. Why is that? Because staying ahead of real estate's evolution is how I maximize its potential as a wealth-building asset.

Owning real estate is about playing the long game. It's not just bricks and mortar—it's a strategy for growing, protecting, and passing on wealth. When you buy property, you're stepping into this tradition, securing your place in a story that's been unfolding for millennia.

Where Real Estate Was

Imagine standing at the heart of an ancient empire in which they didn't measure power in gold or armies, but in land. The most formidable rulers didn't just expand their territories, but they also secured the fertile valleys and bustling trade routes that sustained entire civilizations. Land was the gold mine of its time—feeding populations, fueling economies, and ensuring prosperity for those who possessed it.

Centuries later, in medieval Europe, the power of land remained undeniable. Nobles and landlords didn't just own vast estates, but they also provided structure, protection, and opportunity. Farmers and craftsmen worked the land, producing food and goods that supported the local economy. In return, they had security, a place to live, and the chance to build a better life. Landownership represented more than just control; it was a system of mutual dependence that ensured shared prosperity and thriving communities.

Then came the Industrial Revolution, and with it, a seismic shift. The countryside, once the heart of wealth, gave way to bustling cities. As factories rose and populations swelled, land in urban centers became the new epicenter of opportunity. Those who owned real estate in the right places didn't just amass wealth, but they also shaped the future—providing homes, workplaces, and infrastructure for a transforming world.

Across history, land has remained the foundation of prosperity. Whether feeding nations, supporting livelihoods, or driving industrial growth, those who understood its value weren't just powerful— they were the architects of progress. Through it all, one fact has remained constant: those who own property hold the upper hand. Real estate is more than a resource—it has been and is the foundation of survival, security, and status.

Where Real Estate Is Now

Real estate has long been a cornerstone of wealth, but its influence has grown far beyond individual ownership. In today's world, urban growth has made cities the epicenters of economic activity, and owning property in prime urban or suburban areas has become a key strategy for capitalizing on population growth and rising demand. More than just a financial asset, real estate holds deep social significance. A home represents pride, stability, and the chance to leave a lasting legacy. Economically, its impact is profound, driving job creation, generating rental income, and funding essential infrastructure through property taxes. In this dynamic era, real estate is no longer just about owning land; it's also about leveraging opportunities, adapting to societal needs, and creating wealth in innovative ways that shape our communities and futures.

Where Real Estate Is Headed

Change is the law of life. And those who look only to the past or present are certain to miss the future.

— JOHN F. KENNEDY

The future of real estate is being shaped by three transformative forces, each offering unique opportunities for investors who are ready to adapt. First, urbanization is redefining where people live and work. Experts predict that nearly 70 percent of the global population will live in cities by 2050; however, suburbs are also experiencing a renaissance as families prioritize affordability and space. Savvy investors who tap into these shifting demographics can position themselves for significant growth.

Second, sustainability is no longer optional—it's essential. Green building practices and eco-friendly homes are gaining traction as buyers and renters increasingly demand energy efficiency and environmental responsibility. Properties that embrace these principles not only reduce costs but also enhance long-term value.

Finally, technology is revolutionizing the industry. Innovations such as blockchain are simplifying property transactions, virtual tours are enhancing the buyer experience, and smart home systems are creating more efficient, connected living spaces. Staying informed about these advancements isn't just smart—it's necessary.

As an investor, I'm not just observing these changes; I'm embracing them. Whether it's exploring blockchain for seamless transactions or leveraging AI tools for sharper market insights, I'm committed to staying ahead of the curve. Why? Because in the world of real estate, adapting to change is the key to unlocking the full potential of this incredible asset.

The Enduring Worth of Real Estate

The lasting value of real estate lies in its tangible and enduring nature, setting it apart from volatile assets like stocks or cryptocurrencies. Unlike digital or paper investments that can evaporate in a market crash, real estate is real—something you can see, touch, and use. It fulfills a fundamental human need: shelter.

Of course, no investment is without risk. The 2008–2009 housing crash remains fresh in many minds, serving as a reminder that real estate markets can experience downturns. However, history has proven real estate resilience. Despite market cycles, property values have not only recovered but have reached new highs. Over time, real estate has shown a unique ability to appreciate, outpacing inflation and creating generational wealth.

But real estate is more than just an investment; it's a legacy. Owning property means building something that can outlive you, providing security and opportunity for future generations. This blend of practicality, stability, and long-term growth makes real estate an unmatched cornerstone of wealth—one that continues to stand the test of time.

Key Takeaways

As you embark on your real estate journey, remember that you're stepping into a tradition that has shaped wealth and influence for centuries, while also embracing a future full of potential. Real estate isn't static—it's a dynamic, ever-evolving asset, and those who understand its shifts and opportunities are the ones who reap the greatest rewards. Whether you're investing in a single-family home, exploring the possibilities of green housing, or leveraging cutting-edge technologies, adapting to change and making informed decisions will be key to long-term success. This journey is about more than just owning property—it's about building freedom, security, and opportunity for yourself and those who come after you. And that transformative legacy begins with the choices you make today.

CHAPTER 3: THE BENEFITS OF REAL ESTATE AS AN ASSET

R eal estate isn't just numbers on a screen. Unlike stocks or bonds, it's a tangible, physical asset—you can touch it, see it, and improve it. That tangibility gives real estate unique advantages, offering security and control that paper assets can't match.

But what really makes real estate powerful isn't just the fact that it's tangible. It's the fact that it allows you to build wealth in multiple ways at once. Let's break down the five key financial benefits every investor should know:

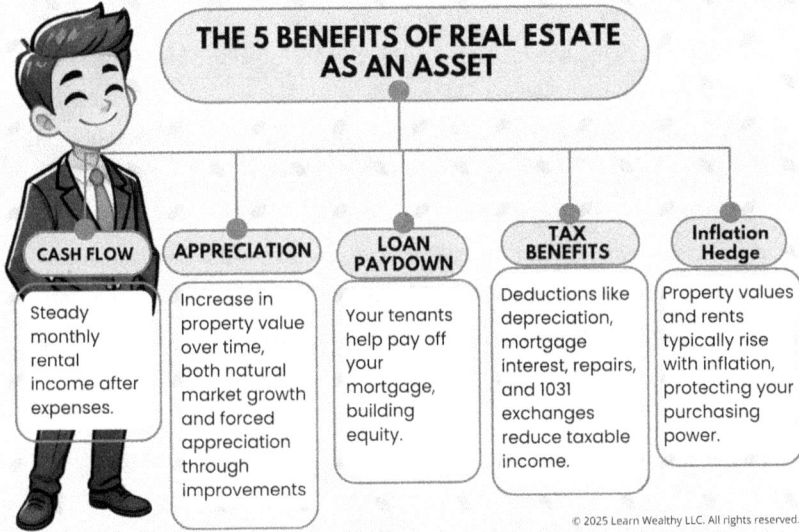

THE 5 BENEFITS OF REAL ESTATE AS AN ASSET

CASH FLOW	APPRECIATION	LOAN PAYDOWN	TAX BENEFITS	Inflation Hedge
Steady monthly rental income after expenses.	Increase in property value over time, both natural market growth and forced appreciation through improvements	Your tenants help pay off your mortgage, building equity.	Deductions like depreciation, mortgage interest, repairs, and 1031 exchanges reduce taxable income.	Property values and rents typically rise with inflation, protecting your purchasing power.

The 5 Benefits of Real Estate as an Asset

Each of these benefits plays a unique role in strengthening your financial foundation. The magic happens when you combine them: rental income flowing in monthly, your tenants paying down your mortgage, and your property appreciating—all while you enjoy significant tax advantages and the natural hedge against inflation.

In the sections ahead, we'll break down each benefit in detail so you can see exactly how to leverage them and maximize your returns.

Why Real Estate Is Considered a Stable and Reliable Investment

One of the key reasons investors turn to real estate is its unique stability. Unlike stocks or cryptocurrencies, which can experience extreme volatility, real estate remains a trusted asset class that provides security, consistent demand, and long-term resilience.

During the 2008 financial crash, Michael watched his stock portfolio plummet by 50 percent overnight. Years of careful investing disappeared in *a matter of months. Frustrated by the market's volatility, he shifted his focus to real estate. Instead of buying stocks, he purchased a modest rental home in a growing suburban area for $180,000. While stock prices continued to swing wildly, his property remained steady—his tenants paid rent every month, covering his mortgage and expenses. Over the next decade, as the economy recovered, his home's value rose to $320,000. On top of that, he had collected more than $80,000 in rental income. Unlike stocks, where he had no control, Michael realized that real estate gave him a stable, income-producing asset that grew over time—one he could see and touch. That single investment transformed his entire wealth-building strategy, proving that real estate wasn't just another asset, but it was a financial foundation.*

A major advantage of real estate is its tangible nature. Unlike digital or paper investments, property is something you can see, touch, and even use. As Donald Trump once put it, *"In real estate, you can feel it, you can touch it, and if things go wrong, you can live in it."* This physical presence gives investors a sense of security that other assets simply can't match.

Beyond its tangibility, real estate holds value because it meets a fundamental human need—shelter. While speculative investments can soar or crash based on market sentiment, the demand for housing remains steady. Even during economic downturns, people still need places to live, work, and do business. Unlike tech stocks that may nose-dive in a bear market, real estate continues to serve a practical purpose, making it a reliable store of value.

Additionally, real estate tends to be less volatile than other investments. While property values can decline during economic crises, they generally recover over time. For example, the 2008 financial crash saw sharp declines in real estate prices. However, within a decade, most markets not only rebounded but reached new highs—proving real estate's resilience over the long term.

These qualities—tangibility, essential demand, and stability—make real estate a cornerstone of wealth-building, offering a level of security that few other assets can provide.

Appreciation over Time: One of the most attractive aspects of real estate is appreciation—the increase in a property's value over time. This growth can happen in two primary ways: naturally through market conditions or intentionally through strategic improvements.

Natural appreciation occurs when external factors drive up property values. Population growth, economic expansion, and rising demand for housing in key areas all contribute to this. Homes near thriving job markets, new infrastructure projects, or highly rated schools often see significant gains without the owner making any changes.

Forced appreciation happens when an investor takes an active role in increasing a property's value. Consider Sarah, who purchased a home for $200,000 and invested $20,000 in upgrading the kitchen and bathrooms. Within a year, her home was appraised at $250,000, creating $50,000 in additional equity. That's a 250 percent return on her renovation investment—proof that well-planned improvements can dramatically boost a property's worth.

Whether appreciation happens naturally or through strategic effort, understanding how to leverage it is a key component of successful real estate investing.

Income Generation: While appreciation builds wealth over time, real estate's real superpower is its ability to put money in your pocket every month. Unlike stocks, where profits are only realized when you sell, rental income provides immediate, steady cash flow—turning your property into a long-term income-generating asset. One of the primary ways investors earn from real estate is through rental income. Monthly rent payments help offset expenses such as mortgages, property taxes, and maintenance. When rental income exceeds these costs, the property produces positive cash flow, meaning it's not just paying for itself, but it is also putting money in the owner's pocket.

For those investing in commercial real estate, leases offer another layer of financial stability. Long-term leases, like those with corporate tenants for five years, provide a more predictable income and lower turnover costs. While no lease can offer absolute certainty—especially in today's shifting commercial landscape—longer contracts generally provide more stability than shorter-term agreements.

As Russell Sage once said, *"Real estate is an imperishable asset, ever increasing in value. It is the most solid security that human ingenuity has devised."* With its ability to generate both income and appreciation, real estate remains one of the most reliable paths to financial security.

Loan Pay-Down by Tenants and Inflation Erosion: One of the hidden advantages of real estate investing is that your tenants help pay down your mortgage. With every rent payment, a portion goes toward reducing your loan balance, steadily increasing your equity over time. In essence, you're building wealth with someone else's money—an opportunity rarely found in other investments.

Beyond this, inflation plays a crucial role in eroding the real cost of debt. Borrowing $200,000 today may feel like a significant burden, but thanks to inflation, that same amount will feel much smaller in twenty years. Meanwhile, your property value and rental income are likely to rise, making the debt even easier to manage.

For example, if inflation averages 3 percent per year and your mortgage interest rate is 5 percent, your real interest rate—adjusted for inflation—is effectively just 2 percent. At the same time, if your property appreciates at an annual rate of 4–6 percent, you're not only outpacing inflation but you are also growing your wealth significantly. This combination of tenant-assisted loan pay-down and inflation-driven debt erosion makes real estate one of the most powerful long-term investments available.

Tax Advantages and Leveraging Potential: One of the most powerful aspects of real estate investing is its tax benefits, which can significantly enhance returns. Investors can deduct key expenses such as property taxes, mortgage interest, repairs, and maintenance, reducing taxable income. Depreciation provides another major advantage—it allows investors to claim a tax deduction on the property's wear and tear, even as the property itself appreciates in value.

For those looking to scale their investments, the 1031 Exchange is a game-changer. This provision allows investors to defer capital gains taxes by reinvesting profits from one property into another, enabling wealth to grow tax-deferred rather than being diminished by immediate taxation.

Beyond tax benefits, real estate also offers unmatched leverage—the ability to control high-value assets with borrowed money. By putting as little as 20 percent down, investors can reap the full benefits of appreciation and rental income on the entire property. But leverage doesn't stop at the purchase. As a property builds equity, investors can tap into that value through a home equity loan, a HELOC (Home Equity Line of Credit), or a cash-out refinance. The best part? Funds accessed through these methods aren't considered taxable income, allowing investors to reinvest without losing a significant portion to taxes.

As T. Harv Eker wisely put it, *"Don't wait to buy real estate. Buy real estate and wait."* With its combination of tax advantages and financial leverage, real estate remains one of the most powerful tools for building and preserving wealth over time.

Comparing Real Estate with Other Asset Classes

Real estate stands apart from other asset classes because of its unique combination of benefits that many alternatives lack. Unlike stocks or cryptocurrencies, which are intangible and subject to extreme market volatility, real estate is a tangible asset with intrinsic value that isn't tied solely to market sentiment. While stocks and bonds can provide income through dividends or interest, rental income from real estate often offers higher cash flow potential with less daily price fluctuation. Cryptocurrencies, though revolutionary, lack the stability and historical appreciation that real estate provides. The ability to use leverage safely in real estate—such as obtaining a mortgage to buy a property—outshines the risks of leveraging in stocks, which can lead to devastating losses during market downturns. Real estate also provides unmatched tax benefits, including deductions for expenses such as mortgage interest, depreciation, and the ability to defer taxes through tools like the 1031 Exchange. These advantages are often absent or less pronounced in other asset classes, making real estate a compelling and versatile investment choice.

Key Takeaways

Real estate isn't just an investment; it's a wealth-building engine that works for you in multiple ways at once. With appreciation growing your equity, rental income generating steady cash flow, tenants paying down your mortgage, and tax advantages maximizing your returns, no other asset class offers this level of financial leverage. Whether you're looking to build long-term security or create a legacy of wealth, real estate remains one of the smartest and most dependable investments available.

As you continue to explore single-family real estate, you'll see why it's considered one of the best ways to build and preserve wealth over time.

CHAPTER 4: TYPES OF REAL ESTATE INVESTMENT STRATEGIES

R eal estate investing offers a variety of strategies to suit different goals, budgets, and levels of experience. In this chapter, we'll explore the most common types of real estate investments, their key characteristics, and the pros and cons of each—especially for beginners.

Buying and Holding Properties

Overview: Buying and holding involves purchasing a property and keeping it long-term while renting it out to generate income. This strategy allows investors to enjoy the full spectrum of real estate benefits.

How It Works: The buy-and-hold strategy is one of the most powerful wealth-building methods in real estate. It is simple yet incredibly effective: you purchase a property—whether it's a single-family home, multifamily unit, or commercial space—with the goal of holding on to it for the long haul. Once rented out, it generates a steady stream of income, covering expenses while putting extra cash in your pocket. But here's where the real magic happens—as the mortgage gets paid down, your equity grows, and thanks to appreciation, the property's value increases over time. Unlike stocks or other investments in which you rely solely on market speculation, buy-and-hold real estate lets you benefit from multiple wealth-building forces at once: rental income, appreciation, loan pay-down, tax advantages, and inflation resistance. It's no surprise that this strategy is a cornerstone of real estate investing, providing stability, long-term financial growth, and an unmatched path to financial freedom.

A First-Time Investor's Journey – From Hesitation to Wealth: *When Sarah first considered real estate investing, she had no idea where to start. She'd always heard that real estate was a smart way to build wealth, but the thought of flipping houses or managing tenants felt overwhelming to her. With a modest budget and little experience, she dipped her toes in with a single-family rental—a buy-and-hold property in a growing neighborhood. She found a three-bedroom home in a good school district, secured a conventional loan, and rented it out to a young family. The first few months weren't without challenges—a leaky faucet here, a late rent payment there—but she quickly learned that with a solid lease and a reliable handyman, most issues were easy to manage.*

Fast forward five years, and Sarah's property had not only paid for itself with rental income, but had also appreciated by $80,000. She refinanced, pulled equity out, and used it to buy a second rental—this time, a duplex. With two properties under her belt, she started seeing the true power of buy-and-hold investing. The best part? Her tenants were paying down her mortgages while her properties continued to grow in value. What started as a hesitant step into real estate had now turned into a full-fledged wealth-building strategy. Sarah no longer feared real estate—she embraced it.

Why It Is the Ultimate Strategy: One of the biggest advantages of buy-and-hold investing is its ability to grow in value in two ways: natural appreciation and forced appreciation. Natural appreciation happens as population growth, economic expansion, and increasing demand push property values higher over time. But savvy investors don't just wait—they actively increase their property's worth through forced appreciation, making strategic renovations and upgrades that instantly boost market value. This combination allows buy-and-hold investors to build wealth exponentially.

Beyond appreciation, buy-and-hold investing offers a powerful combination of financial benefits that make it a wealth-building powerhouse. Investors enjoy major tax advantages, such as deductions on mortgage interest and property depreciation, which significantly lower taxable income. Meanwhile, consistent rental income generates steady cash flow, covering expenses and leaving profits each month. Over time, tenants effectively pay down your mortgage, steadily building your equity with each rent check. Even inflation works in your favor. As property values and rents rise, your loan remains fixed, meaning you're paying back yesterday's debt with tomorrow's stronger dollars. This combination of cash flow, equity growth, and inflation resistance makes buy-and-hold real estate one of the most reliable paths to long-term financial security.

Pros and Cons for Beginners in Real Estate Investing: Real estate offers a powerful wealth-building opportunity, but it comes with its own set of challenges. On the positive side, it provides comprehensive wealth-building, giving investors access to benefits such as appreciation, tax advantages, and equity growth. Rental properties generate steady income, offering a reliable cash flow month after month. Additionally, real estate offers long-term security as it builds equity over time and serves as a hedge against inflation.

However, beginners should also know the challenges. Managing real estate is time-consuming, demanding property management and tenant oversight, although outsourcing these tasks reduces the burden. The up-front costs can be significant, with down payments and closing costs often posing a financial hurdle. Last, there is always market risk, as property values can stagnate or even decline during economic downturns. Understanding both the advantages and challenges is essential for anyone starting their real estate journey.

Fix-and-Flip

Overview: This strategy involves purchasing distressed properties at a low price, renovating them, and selling them for a profit within a short time frame.

How It Works: The fix-and-flip strategy is a dynamic approach to real estate investing that focuses on buying undervalued properties, adding value through improvements, and selling them for a profit. The process begins with identifying properties in promising neighborhoods that are priced below market value, often due to neglect or the need for updates. Once purchased, the property undergoes renovations or remodeling to enhance its market appeal and significantly increase its value. This could include anything from cosmetic upgrades like fresh paint and new flooring to larger projects like kitchen remodels or structural repairs. The key to success lies in completing the renovations efficiently and managing costs to maximize the return on investment. Once the upgrades are complete, the property is listed for sale, with the goal of selling quickly to capitalize on the improved value and turn a profit. This strategy requires a keen eye for market trends, a solid understanding of renovation costs, and the ability to execute projects on time and within budget. When done right, it can be a lucrative way to build wealth in real estate.

Advantages and Disadvantages of House Flipping for Beginners: The fix-and-flip strategy offers an exciting opportunity for beginners, but it comes with both significant advantages and challenges. On the positive side, it boasts high profit potential, as a successful flip can generate substantial returns in a relatively short period. It also provides a hands-on learning experience, teaching practical skills in construction, budgeting, and market analysis. This strategy involves no long-term commitment, as you're not tied to the property for years. However, beginners should be prepared for the challenges. Taxes can eat into profits, as earnings are subject to short-term capital gains rates. There is also holding risk; expenses such as mortgage payments, taxes, and utilities can pile up if the property doesn't sell quickly. Market risk is another factor to consider; a market downturn during your project could cause difficulty selling, or even financial losses. Finally, flipping is capital intensive, requiring substantial up-front cash or access to financing. For those willing to navigate these challenges, the fix-and-flip strategy can be a profitable way to break into real estate investing.

Real Estate Investment Trusts (REITs)

Overview: REITs are companies that own, operate, or finance income-generating real estate. They're one of the easiest ways to invest in real estate without directly owning property.

How It Works: Real Estate Investment Trusts (REITs) provide an accessible and convenient way to invest in real estate without the challenges of directly owning or managing properties. REITs can be either publicly traded on stock exchanges or privately held, offering investors flexibility in choosing how to participate. By purchasing shares in a REIT, investors gain exposure to a professionally managed portfolio of income-generating properties, which can include residential, commercial, industrial, or even specialized real estate like healthcare facilities or data centers. These properties generate rental income or profits from sales, which are then distributed to shareholders in the form of dividends. One of the key advantages of REITs is diversification, as they spread investments across various property types and locations, reducing risk while still offering the potential for stable returns. For investors seeking a passive way to participate in the real estate market, REITs combine the benefits of real estate ownership with the liquidity and accessibility of traditional stock market investments.

Pros and Cons for Beginners: Investing in Real Estate Investment Trusts (REITs) offers several advantages for beginners but also comes with its share of challenges. On the positive side, REITs provide easy entry into real estate investing, with some IPOs and shares available for as little as sixteen dollars, making them accessible to almost anyone. They also offer decent dividend yields, typically ranging between 4 and 7 percent, providing a reliable source of passive income. Another major benefit is that REIT investors face no property-management responsibilities, avoiding the headaches of tenant oversight or maintenance. Publicly traded REITs are highly liquid, allowing investors to buy and sell shares on the stock market with ease, unlike physical properties, which can take months to transact.

However, there are drawbacks to consider. Investors have no

control over property management, acquisitions, or strategies, leaving these decisions entirely in the hands of the REIT managers. Due diligence is critical for wise investing, as it requires understanding the company's financial health, debt levels, cash flow, and future outlook, as well as being aware of the property sectors the REIT focuses on, such as residential, commercial, or industrial. REITs are also subject to market volatility, with share prices fluctuating based on broader economic conditions. Finally, taxable dividends can diminish returns, as they are taxed as ordinary income. For beginners, REITs can be an excellent way to enter the real estate market, but it's essential to weigh these pros and cons carefully.

MOST STRATEGIES—LIKE buy-and-hold or fix-and-flip—can apply to any of these property types. Here's a quick comparison of how they differ:

Real Estate Investment Comparisons

Category	Initial Capital Needed	Risk	Cash Flow	Management Effort
Single Family	Often lower down payment; easier loan access	Market demand for SFH is stable; easier to rent or sell	Can cash flow well with proper purchase price and rent balance	Manage yourself or hire a property manager
Multifamily	More units = higher purchase price; may need stronger finances	Vacancies spread over more units, but management complexity increases	More units = more rent sources; often strong cash flow	Time-intensive unless you hire help
Commercial	Typically requires large upfront investment; complex underwriting	Tenant turnover, economic cycles, and longer vacancies increase risk	Can generate high returns but harder to stabilize	Very complex leases and operations; usually outsourced
REITS	Buy shares with as little as $20; no property purchase required	Risk is diversified across many properties and markets	Modest dividends; no direct rent collection	No management required; fully passive

How different property types compare across key investment factors

Which Strategy Is Best for Beginners?

As a beginner primarily looking to invest in single-family homes, it's essential to understand the key strategies for real estate investing. While your focus might be on single-family properties, knowing about other options, such as REITs, broadens your perspective and helps you make informed decisions about your investment journey.

If you're an active learner eager to gain hands-on experience, strategies such as buying and holding single-family homes or taking on fix-and-flip projects are ideal. These approaches immerse you in every aspect of real estate investing, from analyzing deals to managing properties, and help you build valuable skills in running a real estate business.

For passive investors, REITs and buy-and-hold strategies offer excellent options. REITs provide a completely hands-off way to invest in real estate, while buy-and-hold can evolve into a passive investment over time. Initially, managing single-family rentals may require effort as you learn the ropes, build systems, and assemble a reliable team. However, once these elements are in place, buy-and-hold investments can become relatively passive and provide steady cash flow.

If you're a budget-conscious beginner, REITs are a great way to start. They require significantly less up-front capital compared with purchasing single-family homes and allow you to dip your toes into real estate investing without the financial burden of down payments, closing costs, or maintenance expenses.

Ultimately, the best strategy for you depends on your goals, resources, and the level of involvement you're ready to commit to. As a beginner focused on single-family homes, buying and holding properties is a powerful long-term strategy that combines wealth-building, cash flow, and eventual passivity once you've established your systems.

Key Takeaways

The buy-and-hold strategy stands out as the most comprehensive path to long-term wealth, combining all the key benefits of real estate: appreciation, tax advantages, cash flow, loan pay-down, and return on amortization (loan erosion through inflation). However, every investment strategy has its strengths and weaknesses, and the best choice depends on your goals, resources, and risk tolerance.

The most important part of real estate isn't the properties themselves or the strategies you use; it's you and your goals as an investor. Real estate investing isn't a one-size-fits-all approach. What works for one person may not work for another, and your unique circumstances, preferences, and objectives will guide your decisions.

As you gain experience and become efficient in one strategy, you can even explore multiple strategies to diversify and expand your portfolio. However, the key to long-term success lies in mastering at least one approach before branching out.

Whether you prefer the hands-on approach of flipping properties or the passive income of REITs, real estate offers diverse investment opportunities. In the next chapter, we'll dive into economics and how it affects real estate investments.

CHAPTER 5: THE ECONOMICS OF REAL ESTATE

The real estate market operates within the framework of basic economic principles, primarily driven by supply and demand. Understanding these principles, along with the factors that influence property values and the cyclical nature of the market, is crucial for making informed investment decisions.

"The first lesson of economics is scarcity: There is never enough of anything to satisfy all those who want it."

— THOMAS SOWELL

This concept of scarcity is particularly relevant in real estate, where limited supply and varying demand create opportunities and challenges for investors. In this chapter, we'll break down how real estate economics work and why timing and strategy are key to success.

Supply and Demand in Real Estate Markets

At its core, the price of real estate is determined by the balance (or imbalance) between supply and demand. Let's examine these forces in detail.

In real estate, supply refers to the number of properties available for sale or rent in a given market, and it has a huge impact on prices and demand. Unlike other markets, real estate is limited by geography—there's only so much land, and prime locations are even scarcer. Add to this zoning laws, development restrictions, and local regulations, and the supply becomes even more constrained. While new construction can help ease the pressure, it's not a quick fix. Building homes or developments takes time, money, and coordination, which often means new supply can't keep up with growing demand, especially in booming areas.

Take cities like San Francisco or New York as prime examples of how supply constraints play out. Limited land, strict zoning rules, and resistance to new development have kept housing supply tight, driving prices sky-high. This shortage creates affordability challenges that ripple across the market. Understanding this balance between supply and demand is key to seeing why real estate remains such a valuable and dynamic investment.

Demand in real estate refers to the desire and ability of buyers or renters to purchase or lease property, and it's influenced by various factors, such as economic conditions, job growth, consumer preferences, and even external events. A great example is the rise of remote work during the COVID-19 pandemic, which reshaped housing markets as families left urban centers for suburban or rural areas, seeking more space and affordability.

However, demand isn't just about wanting a property; it's also about having the means to act on that desire. True demand requires both the motivation and the financial ability to purchase or rent. This means that buyers or renters need sufficient resources, legal qualifications, and logistical readiness to turn interest into action. Understanding this balance is key to analyzing how market trends and economic shifts influence real estate demand.

The Importance of Financial and Legal Viability

Imagine a region attracting a surge of newcomers—perhaps for job opportunities, natural beauty, or other appealing factors. At first glance, this might seem like a recipe for skyrocketing housing demand. After all, more people usually means more need for housing, right? Historically, population growth and rising real estate demand often go hand in hand, but the connection isn't always so simple.

Take this example: if the new arrivals can't afford housing or don't have the legal status to buy property, their presence doesn't translate into actual demand. Similarly, tourists might dream of owning a home in the area, but their temporary status or local laws often make it impossible. Without the right mix of financial resources, legal clearance, and paperwork, those desires stay just that—dreams. And unfortunately, dreams don't move the housing market.

The Balance of Supply and Demand

Real estate markets are driven by the delicate balance of supply and demand, with "price" acting as the fulcrum. When demand surpasses supply, prices tend to rise, sometimes dramatically, as buyers compete for limited properties. This often leads to bidding wars, soaring home values, and a seller's market. When supply exceeds demand, prices stagnate or decline because sellers must lower their asking prices to attract buyers, creating a buyer's market.

The concept of "equilibrium" in real estate refers to when supply and demand are balanced and prices remain stable. However, equilibrium is rarely static in this dynamic market. The balance is constantly shifting because of factors such as interest rates, job growth, local development, and economic health. For instance, a drop in mortgage rates can spur demand, pushing prices higher if supply doesn't keep up. Conversely, an oversupply of new construction in a slowing economy can lead to falling prices, even if demand remains steady.

Price acts as the mechanism that adjusts supply and demand toward equilibrium. When prices rise too high, fewer buyers can afford to enter the market, tempering demand. Meanwhile, higher prices often reward sellers, encouraging homeowners to list properties or developers to build more homes, gradually increasing supply. Conversely, when prices drop, demand can increase as homes become more affordable, while supply may shrink as sellers hold off for better market conditions. Understanding this interplay between supply, demand, price, and equilibrium is essential for navigating the ever-changing real estate landscape.

Personal Reflection on Location and Lifestyle Tradeoffs

As I reflect on the importance of supply and demand in real estate, I'm reminded of my personal experiences in the Philippines. I grew up there, and in 2022, I revisited some of the most stunning tropical paradises, such as Boracay and Siargao. The beauty of these beaches was exhilarating—crystal-clear waters, powdery white sand, and serene sunsets that seemed to stretch forever.

At first glance, it felt like the perfect place to buy property and live happily ever after by the sea. However, reality often challenges our dreams. These picturesque locations, while breathtaking, lack the availability of jobs and opportunities for building wealth. If you are someone who thrives in the hustle and bustle of big cities, with their access to thriving job markets, large communities, and modern amenities like major hospitals and shopping centers, these islands might not be as desirable.

It's a trade-off that real estate investors and buyers must often make. Do you prioritize the serene beauty of a remote location or the practical advantages of a well-connected urban hub? The answer depends on your lifestyle goals and financial aspirations. Understanding this balance is a critical part of making informed real estate decisions.

Additional Factors Influencing Property Value

A combination of tangible and intangible factors shapes the value of real estate. Understanding these influences can provide investors with the clarity needed to make informed decisions.

The timeless rule of real estate—"Location, location, location"—remains a cornerstone of the industry. However, there is a deeper truth: it's not the location itself that holds value, but the people who value it. Real estate, at its core, exists to serve people. Without people who recognize, desire, and are willing to pay for a location's benefits, even the most idyllic spots hold little economic value.

At its core, the value of real estate lies in its ability to meet the needs of people. It's not just about land or buildings, but it's also about how well a location serves the individuals and communities who interact with it. Therefore, some places command premium prices while others remain undervalued. The power of location doesn't exist in isolation; it's driven by the people who recognize and value its benefits.

Proximity to amenities such as schools, parks, transportation hubs, and employment centers plays a significant role in shaping demand and pricing. These features are valuable only because people see them as beneficial. Factors such as neighborhood safety, walkability, and future development plans can further enhance a property's appeal, but its importance lies in how well it addresses the needs and desires of potential buyers or renters.

Not all locations are equally desirable. Some areas attract a large group of people willing and able to pay a premium, making them far more valuable than others. While land is finite, it is only truly scarce in regions where demand exists. Vast stretches of unused land often remain overlooked because they lack the infrastructure, access, and community features that make them desirable to people.

Understanding this human-centric perspective is essential in real estate. To truly evaluate a location's potential, it is not enough to consider its features; you must also assess the people it appeals to and their ability to act on that desire. Ultimately, real estate isn't just about places; it's also about the people who bring those places to life.

Desirability Defines Scarcity

Land without access to cities, utilities, groceries, or a sense of community is rarely in demand. Such areas might hold value for industrial purposes, but for residential or commercial real estate, their isolation makes them irrelevant to most buyers.

In contrast, specific locations such as beachfront properties, historic neighborhoods, or ultra-safe communities derive value from their unique features. These places are not inherently valuable on their own, but they become desirable because they attract people who highly value their characteristics.

Beachfront properties, for instance, offer a combination of natural beauty and limited availability, resulting in exclusivity. Similarly, families seek neighborhoods with top-rated schools, a strong safety record, and a vibrant community because they view them as ideal places to raise children. The more people who value and compete for these areas, the more the location's value increases.

The Impact of Rate Changes

Interest rates play a significant role in determining property values by directly influencing affordability. When interest rates are low, buyers gain more purchasing power because they can borrow money at a lower cost. This often drives up demand and leads to higher home prices. Conversely, when interest rates rise, the cost of borrowing increases, making monthly payments more expensive. As afford-ability declines, demand cools—which can lead to stagnation or even a drop in home prices.

Consider a buyer with a $2,000 monthly budget for housing:

- At a 3 percent interest rate, they can afford a home priced at $500,000.
- At a 6 percent interest rate, that same monthly budget only allows for a home priced at $375,000.

This shows why even minor changes in interest rates can significantly shift buyer behavior and overall market conditions.

The Ripple Effect of Interest Rates

Changes in interest rates don't just affect individual buyers, but they ripple through the entire market. Low rates stimulate demand, encouraging buyers to enter the market and developers to build more properties. High rates can suppress demand, slow construction, and lead to an oversupply of homes. Investors who monitor interest rate trends can position themselves to capitalize on these fluctuations.

Understanding the Federal Reserve's Role

The Federal Reserve, or the Fed, plays a critical role in shaping the broader economic landscape and the real estate market. By adjusting the federal funds rate—the interest rate that banks charge each other for overnight loans—the Fed seeks to influence economic activity. These adjustments aim to control inflation, stimulate economic growth, or respond to financial crises.

However, while the federal funds rate primarily affects short-term loans such as car loans or credit card debts, its impact on mortgage rates is secondary. Mortgage rates are driven by a different mechanism that investors need to understand.

The Key Driver: The 10-Year Treasury Yield

Do you ever wonder why mortgage rates go up and down? It's not just because of what the Federal Reserve does. The real key player here is the 10-year Treasury yield. This yield shows the return investors get when they buy 10-year U.S. Treasury bonds, which are considered super safe investments. Since both mortgages and these bonds are long-term commitments with similar risks, mortgage rates tend to follow the 10-year Treasury yield.

Here is how it works:

- When the 10-year Treasury yield goes up, mortgage rates also rise. This makes borrowing more expensive for homebuyers.
- When the yield drops, mortgage rates fall too, making it cheaper to get a loan and buy a house.

Why does this happen? Mortgage-backed securities (MBS), bundles of home loans sold to investors, fund most mortgages. These investors look at the 10-year Treasury yield as a guide. If Treasury yields rise, investors want higher returns on MBS, which pushes mortgage rates up. When Treasury yields fall, mortgage rates go down too.

Additional Factors That Shape the Real Estate Market

Demographics play a big role in long-term demand. Growing populations, including younger families seeking suburban homes and retirees seeking low-maintenance living, create diverse housing demands. Migration patterns also matter, as cities with job opportunities and a great lifestyle, like Austin, Texas, often see rising home prices.

Economic conditions are another key player. When the economy is strong, with low unemployment and higher wages, more people can afford homes, boosting demand. On the flip side, recessions can slow the market, causing prices to stall or drop.

Then there are external influences, such as natural disasters, that can reshape local markets by reducing supply or shifting demand. Government policies, like new zoning laws or tax breaks, can also heat up or cool down the market. Even global events such as pandemics or geopolitical conflicts can affect everything from migration to construction costs. Together, these forces create the dynamic world of real estate, where supply, demand, and prices are always in motion.

The Case-Shiller Index: A Tool for Understanding Real Estate Trends

The Case-Shiller Index, created by economists Karl Case and Robert Shiller, is one of the most widely recognized tools for tracking real estate market trends. It measures the changes in home prices across the United States, providing a broad and reliable view of how the housing market is performing over time.

This index specifically tracks repeat sales of the same homes to determine price trends. By focusing on repeat sales, it eliminates much of the noise caused by variations in property types or sizes. As a result, the Case-Shiller Index offers a more accurate measure of housing price appreciation or depreciation.

Key Takeaways

The economics of real estate is a fascinating blend of supply-and-demand dynamics, external factors, and cyclical trends. By understanding these principles, you can navigate the market with confidence, recognizing opportunities and avoiding pitfalls. Whether you're analyzing supply constraints, interest rate fluctuations, or the stages of the real estate cycle, this knowledge provides a sound foundation for making informed decisions. As you continue your journey into real estate investing, remember that timing, strategy, and a keen understanding of market forces are your greatest assets.

CHAPTER 6: REAL ESTATE AS A HEDGE AGAINST INFLATION

In the long run, there is no such thing as a fixed value of money. The value of money changes with inflation, and assets like real estate must rise to keep pace.

— ADAPTED FROM LUDWIG VON MISES

Inflation makes things such as groceries and houses more expensive over time, as the value of money shrinks. To protect their money, people look for investments that can keep up with rising prices or even grow in value. Real estate is one of the best choices because it stays steady and often grows in value, even when other investments don't. It helps people hold on to their wealth when prices are rising everywhere.

The House That Kept Getting Pricier

When Mark bought his first rental property, a modest three-bedroom house in a growing suburb, he felt like he had unlocked a secret to wealth. He got it for $200,000, and within a few years, it was worth $300,000. "Real *estate is a cheat code,"* he thought. *Every year, his property value climbed higher, and his net worth followed.*

But as time went on, Mark started noticing something odd.

His property manager raised their fees. "Cost of living is up," they said. The plumber charged nearly double for the same leaky faucet repair. The roof replacement he had been putting off was now 40 percent more expensive. Then came the property tax bill—higher than ever. And his insurance company? "Material costs are rising, so we're adjusting your premium," they explained.

Mark sat at his desk staring at his numbers. His house was worth $350,000 now, but his profits were shrinking. He ran the numbers again. The appreciation felt great, but with every gain, there was a hidden cost waiting to take a bite out of it.

He had fallen for the illusion.

Inflation had boosted his property's price, but it also made everything —management, repairs, taxes, and insurance—more expensive. His real gain wasn't in the rising value of the house, but in how much cash it actually put in his pocket.

That's when it clicked: owning property wasn't just about what it was worth—it was also about what it earned.

And that's the difference between getting rich on paper and getting wealthy in real life.

Inflation Isn't the Cause of Appreciation

It's important to recognize that inflation itself isn't the true driver of real estate appreciation. The real catalyst is the balance of supply and demand. A property's value rises because people want it, and that demand outpaces the supply. Without strong demand, even in inflationary environments, property values can stagnate.

The House That Wasn't Growing

Sam had always felt like a smart investor. He bought his house for
$500,000, and over the years, he watched its value climb past $1 million.
"Real estate is the best investment," he told himself. "It always goes up."
*   But then he had a conversation that shook his confidence.*
*   "Think about it in gold," his friend Chris said. "When you bought this*
place, it cost around 300 ounces. Now? Only 250."
*   Sam frowned. "Wait—so you're saying my house lost value?"*
*   "Not in dollars," Chris said, shrugging. "But in real money? Yeah. Gold*
and Bitcoin have outpaced real estate for years. Your house looks like it's
worth more, but that's just because the dollar keeps getting weaker."
*   Sam sat with that for a moment. He had been measuring wealth in a*
currency that was losing value, mistaking price inflation for real growth.
His house wasn't appreciating—it was just keeping up with a system
designed to devalue the money in his pocket.
*   And suddenly, his million-dollar home didn't seem so impressive*
after all.

Perspective Matters

Ultimately, how you perceive the effects of inflation on real estate
depends on the lens you use. If you measure property values in
devaluing dollars, real estate appears to thrive. But when viewed
through the lens of more sound and appreciating currencies like gold
or Bitcoin, real estate might seem to underperform over time. Understanding this distinction is vital for investors looking to make
informed decisions in an inflationary environment.

The Tug-of-War Between Inflation and Rental Income

On the surface, inflation seems like a gift to landlords. As prices rise
across the economy, rental rates tend to follow, allowing property
owners to collect higher rents and maintain a steady cash flow that

keeps up with the cost of living. A property generating $1,000 in rent today might bring in $1,200 or more in the future, seemingly preserving purchasing power. But while this upward trend looks promising, the reality is far more nuanced.

Higher rents don't materialize simply because inflation exists; they rise when demand does. If an area experiences job growth, an influx of new residents, or rising wages, landlords can charge more because tenants can afford to pay more. But inflation alone doesn't guarantee these conditions. If wages lag behind, tenants struggle to keep up, capping rental increases at what the market can bear.

At the same time, landlords face a growing list of financial pressures. Property-management fees are rising, as are wages. Repair and maintenance costs climb as materials become more expensive. Insurance premiums adjust upward to reflect higher rebuilding costs. Even property taxes swell as home values appreciate. While rental income may grow, so do the expenses that eat into profitability.

The rental market ultimately operates on a delicate balance—what landlords need to charge versus what tenants can afford to pay. Inflation might push numbers higher, but without strong demand and rising incomes to support it, landlords can find themselves caught in a squeeze, where the cost of owning and maintaining a property rises faster than the rents they can collect. In the long run, it's not just about how much rent goes up, but it's about how much actually stays in the investor's pocket.

Studying the Market Over the Property

To effectively navigate these challenges, it's crucial to understand the local rental market and fair market rent. Far more important than knowing the ins and outs of a building is having a clear picture of the following:

- Wages and Employment Trends: Do tenants in the area have increasing incomes to support higher rents?

- Population Growth: Is the area experiencing an influx of new residents, increasing demand for rentals?
- Rental Market Supply: How much competition is there among landlords in the area?

This market knowledge is vital for ensuring that rental properties remain profitable. A property owner who ignores local market trends might face stagnant rental income while simultaneously dealing with higher operating costs, leaving their bottom line worse off, despite nominally higher rents.

The Bottom Line

Inflation can create the illusion of income growth, but without corresponding increases in tenant income and market demand, the benefits of rising rents may be outweighed by increased expenses. Property owners must recognize that supply and demand, not inflation alone, are the true drivers of rental income growth. Studying the market and understanding fair market rent is key to maximizing profitability and avoiding financial pitfalls during inflationary periods.

Fixed-Rate Debt Benefits

For real estate investors with fixed-rate mortgages, inflation can be a powerful ally. While property values and rental income typically rise over time, your loan payments remain fixed, effectively reducing the real cost of your debt. This occurs because inflation erodes the purchasing power of money, making your fixed loan payments feel "cheaper" in the future compared to when you first borrowed the funds.

Example: If you take out a $200,000 loan today, its real cost diminishes over ten or twenty years as inflation reduces the value of the dollar. While your loan balance stays nominally the same, its relative burden shrinks, providing a financial advantage.

The Real Rate of Interest Matters

Your mortgage interest rate is a crucial factor in determining how much inflation benefits you.

- If your mortgage rate is 3 percent and inflation that same year is also 3 percent, the two cancel each other out, resulting in a 0 percent real interest rate for that year. Essentially, inflation negates the cost of borrowing, making your loan cost neutral in real terms.
- If inflation exceeds your mortgage rate, the real cost of borrowing turns negative, further reducing the effective burden of your debt.

The Relationship Between Equity, Loan Balance, and Inflation

Your home's value is made up of two things: your equity (the part you own outright) and your loan balance (what you still owe). For example, if your house is worth $200,000 and you've paid off $100,000, that's your equity; the remaining $100,000 is your loan balance. When inflation happens—let's say it's 10 percent in a year—it means that money overall is worth less because prices for everything go up. This doesn't just affect your loan, but it also affects your equity.

Even though your house might now sell for more in dollars because of inflation, the *real value* of both your loan and your equity —their buying power—is reduced. So if $100,000 could buy a car, a vacation, or a bunch of groceries last year, it won't buy as much this year because inflation has reduced what that money can do. The upside? The loan balance becomes less painful over time because you're paying it back with dollars that are worth less. But the downside is that the same inflation reduces the value of your equity in the same way, so you're not as far ahead as you might think.

The Hidden Battle Between Inflation and Equity—And Why Debt Can Be Your Ally

Imagine this: Your mortgage lender gives you a special deal—you can skip your loan payments for an entire year. No penalties, no extra interest, nothing. Sounds like a dream, right?

You start the year with $100,000 in equity and a $100,000 loan balance on a home worth $200,000. But here's where inflation sneaks in. Over the next twelve months, inflation runs at 10 percent, quietly eroding the value of every dollar you own. By the end of the year, your loan balance still says $100,000, but in real terms, that debt has become cheaper. The same inflation that's making everything else more expensive is actually benefiting you, reducing the burden of what you owe.

But it's not all good news. That $100,000 in equity you had just lost 10 percent of its purchasing power. Your ownership stake in the property may look the same on paper, but in reality, it can now buy less than it could a year ago.

So does inflation make you richer or poorer? That depends on how much debt you hold. If both your loan balance and your equity are eroded by inflation, then holding more debt than equity actually puts you at an advantage. Why? Because inflation eats away at the real value of what you owe, making your debt less costly over time. Meanwhile, your equity—the money you've already put in—shrinks in purchasing power, meaning you're losing value on the part of the home you fully own.

This is why smart investors use leverage in an inflationary environment. Rather than tying up their money in home equity, they use financing to control appreciating assets while letting inflation work in their favor. Over time, as inflation devalues the dollar, their fixed-rate mortgage becomes less of a burden, rents rise, and they build wealth —not just from property appreciation, but from the strategic use of debt.

But don't forget—equity only grows when debt is paid down or when market forces drive appreciation. If supply outpaces demand

and home prices drop, your equity shrinks, no matter how much of the house you own. Inflation inflates numbers, but true wealth in real estate isn't just about rising prices. It's about leveraging debt strategically while ensuring your assets generate income that outpaces inflation. That's how investors position themselves to thrive in an inflationary world.

Key Takeaways

Real estate's role as a hedge against inflation is both nuanced and powerful. While inflation erodes the purchasing power of money, it often drives up property values and rental income, making real estate a reliable asset for preserving and growing wealth. However, as this chapter highlights, the relationship between inflation and real estate is more complex than it seems on the surface.

Inflation provides clear benefits, such as reducing the real cost of fixed-rate debt and creating opportunities for rental income growth. Yet it also introduces challenges, such as rising property-management expenses, maintenance costs, and the erosion of equity. These dynamics emphasize the importance of understanding the true drivers of real estate success: supply and demand.

Ultimately, real estate is not immune to inflation's double-edged sword. The key to thriving as an investor lies in studying market trends, understanding fair market rent, and leveraging tools like fixed-rate debt strategically. By maintaining a long-term perspective and focusing on the fundamentals of supply, demand, and local market conditions, real estate investors can successfully navigate inflationary periods and ensure that their investments remain resilient and profitable.

CHAPTER 7: WHO SHOULD INVEST IN REAL ESTATE?

M any people view real estate as a path to financial freedom, but who is it really for? The answer may surprise you: real estate is an accessible and rewarding investment option for a wide range of individuals, not just for the wealthy or the experienced. In this chapter, we'll explore the types of people who are well-suited to real estate investing, the traits that help investors succeed, and common myths that might hold you back from getting started.

Real estate is the purest form of entrepreneurship.

— BRIAN BUFFINI

Young Professionals: Building Wealth Early

For many young professionals, real estate is the first step toward financial freedom. While renting offers flexibility, it builds no equity; every dollar spent goes into someone else's pocket. Buying a home early is a game changer, transforming a major expense into an investment.

One of the most powerful ways to do this is house hacking, a strategy widely popularized by real estate investor Brandon Turner. It's simple: buy a property, live in one part, and rent out the rest. Whether it's a multiunit building or a home with extra rooms, the rental income can cover a sizable chunk of the mortgage—sometimes all of it—letting you live for free or at a steep discount.

For young professionals without the space demands of a growing family, house hacking is a no-brainer. It prioritizes financial growth over privacy, turning your first home into a wealth-building machine. Instead of waiting years to invest, you start stacking equity, earning passive income, and benefiting from appreciation—all while living in your own home.

Take Sarah, for example. She bought a three-bedroom home, rented out two rooms to friends, and cut her housing costs to nearly zero. In just a few years, rising property values and rental income put her in a position to buy a second property.

By starting early, young professionals can break free from the paycheck-to-paycheck cycle and build a financial future in which their money works for them—not the other way around.

Retirees: Turning Real Estate into a Retirement Safety Net

For many retirees, real estate is more than just an investment—it's a lifeline. A steady stream of rental income can provide financial security in retirement, acting as a reliable supplement to savings and pensions. Unlike the unpredictability of the stock market, a well-managed rental property delivers consistent cash flow, ensuring peace of mind during the golden years.

What is the biggest mistake retirees make? Parking their money in a bank and letting it sit. Retirement can last decades, and with rising healthcare costs and inflation, money that isn't growing is money that's shrinking. The solution? Cash-flowing real estate. A single rental property can turn into an income-producing asset that not only pays the bills but continues to appreciate in value over time.

Consider Robert, a retiree who used part of his savings to buy a fully paid-off rental home. Now, instead of watching his money slowly deplete, he collects a monthly rent check that covers expenses, keeps up with inflation, and provides a financial cushion. His investment isn't just a source of income—it's a safety net that grows instead of disappears.

For retirees, real estate isn't just about making money; it's also about protecting it. With the right investments, retirement can be less about financial stress and more about enjoying life on your own terms.

Entrepreneurs: Building Wealth Like the Ultra rich

For entrepreneurs, real estate isn't just an investment—it's a scalability tool. It funds businesses, provides financial security, and offers leverage to take risks without losing everything. Some of the most successful entrepreneurs didn't just make money from their businesses, but they used real estate to protect and multiply their wealth.

Take Sam Zell, the legendary investor known as the "Grave Dancer" for his ability to find undervalued real estate deals. Zell started small. While still in college, he managed student housing at the University of Michigan. Instead of just collecting rent, he saw an opportunity: he convinced his landlord to let him manage more buildings in exchange for a cut of the profits. Before he even graduated, Zell was running a small real estate empire, making more money than most full-time professionals.

That small start turned into Equity Group Investments, the firm that made Zell one of the richest real estate moguls in history. He scaled his fortune by buying distressed properties, holding on to them while the market rebounded, and selling them for massive profits. Later, he expanded into commercial real estate, office buildings, and industrial properties, creating a multibillion-dollar portfolio that protected his wealth from economic downturns.

Zell's story proves that entrepreneurs who understand real estate aren't just building businesses, but they're building financial fortresses. Whether it's rental properties, commercial spaces, or flipping undervalued assets, real estate provides stability in a world in which businesses rise and fall.

If real estate helped a college student become a billionaire, imagine what it can do for today's entrepreneurs. The question isn't whether real estate is a wonderful investment, but the question is whether you're willing to play the game.

The best part is that you don't have to choose between real estate and your business. The smartest entrepreneurs use real estate to fund their dreams, protect their wealth, and scale their financial future. Whether it's flipping houses for quick capital or holding rentals for long-term stability, real estate is the secret weapon that keeps entrepreneurs in the game—long after the markets shift and trends fade.

Side Hustlers: Turning Part-Time Effort into Full-Time Freedom

For many people with full-time jobs, real estate offers a practical and accessible side hustle. Managing one or two rental properties can be done part-time, providing financial growth without the need to quit a primary job. It's an opportunity to build wealth gradually while maintaining the stability of a steady paycheck.

Let me share a bit of my story here. I could have started young, but I spent a lot of time educating myself first. Despite all that knowledge, I didn't take action to become a real estate agent until 2015, and I didn't buy my first rental property until 2020. But do you know what? That's okay. We all start at different points in life, and it's never too late to make a change.

Back then, being an RN was my full-time career, and real estate was just a side hustle. Today, that's flipped; being an RN is now my side hustle as my real estate portfolio has grown. I've reached the point where I make money while I sleep. At thirty-eight years old, I'm proud of how far I've come, but I know I still have a long way to go. I'm continuing to build my portfolio, and I have started writing books to share my experiences so others can learn and grow along with me.

Now here's the thing: you don't need to be a licensed agent to succeed in real estate. I chose that path because it worked for me, but everybody's journey is different. If you're not planning to represent others or earn commissions, a license isn't necessary. You can handle your own transactions with the right education and resources. Some of the most successful investors focus on one strategy—such as wholesaling, buy-and-hold investing, or house hacking—and get great at it. Many of these strategies don't require a license at all.

The key is to find what works for you and commit to it. Real estate isn't a one-size-fits-all game; it's a versatile field that lets you shape your path to success. So whether you're juggling a full-time job or diving in part-time, remember that small steps can lead to big outcomes. It's all about taking action and building momentum toward your financial freedom.

Example: A schoolteacher might purchase a second home to rent out, creating an additional source of income to support long-term financial goals.

The Traits of a Successful Real Estate Investor

Winning in real estate isn't about luck—it's about mindset, strategy, and the ability to adapt. The best investors don't let setbacks define them. They learn, adjust, and come back stronger.

At its core, real estate is a game of problem-solving. Deals fall apart, tenants become unreliable, repairs cost more than expected— things will go wrong. The difference between a failing investor and a thriving one is how they react. Instead of dwelling on problems, successful investors find solutions, whether it's negotiating better terms, restructuring a deal, or pivoting to a different strategy.

Understanding the numbers is just as important. You don't need to be a math genius, but you must know how cash flow works, how to evaluate risk, and when debt is a tool instead of a burden. Real estate rewards those who trust the numbers rather than emotions.

But the real secret is knowing when to wait and when to move fast. Buy-and-hold investors thrive on patience; time in the market is what builds wealth. Flippers, on the other hand, need urgency—delays eat into profits, and hesitation can turn a great deal into a financial disaster. The best investors understand that timing is everything, and they adjust their approach depending on the deal.

And then there's failure—every investor faces it: the first flip that barely broke even; the rental property that turned into a nightmare; the miscalculated rehab costs. What separates winners from losers is that successful investors learn from mistakes rather than run from them. Every misstep is a lesson, every deal—good or bad—adds experience. Those who embrace setbacks as part of the process become unstoppable.

Finally, real estate is a team sport. The smartest investors don't go at it alone—they build a network of agents, lenders, contractors, and property managers. Knowing the right people can mean the difference between closing a deal and watching it slip away.

Real estate isn't just about properties, but it's about mindset, resilience, and making the right moves at the right time. Those who keep learning, keep solving problems, and keep pushing forward don't just survive the game, but they master it.

Misconceptions: "You Need to Be Rich to Start" and Other Myths

With real estate, many misconceptions prevent people from taking the first step. Let's tackle these myths and set the record straight.

Myth 1: "You Need to Be Rich to Invest in Real Estate."

Reality: Many first-time investors begin with limited funds. Programs like FHA loans allow you to buy a property with as little as 3.5 percent down, making real estate accessible even with modest savings. Creative strategies such as house hacking—where you live in a part of the property while renting out the rest—can further reduce costs. Partnering with others can also lower the financial barriers, allowing you to pool resources and share risks.

Myth 2: "Real Estate Is Too Risky."

Reality: While all investments carry some risk, real estate tends to be more stable than volatile markets like stocks or crypto. With proper research, a focus on cash flow, and investment in desirable locations, you can significantly minimize risks. Unlike other markets, real estate offers tangible assets that retain value even during economic downturns.

Myth 3: "I Need to Know Everything Before I Start."

Reality: Many aspiring investors get stuck in "shiny object syndrome," endlessly researching and jumping from one idea to another without ever taking action. The truth is that no one can know or master everything before they start. Even as portfolios grow, investors eventually form teams to delegate tasks and scale operations. As Robert Kiyosaki once said in a YouTube video, he reached a personal limit on the number of units he could handle and had to partner with Ken McElroy to expand further. Start small, take action, and learn as you go.

Myth 4: "You Need to Invest in Your Own Market."

Reality: You don't need to invest where you live. The key is to invest where the numbers make sense, not where it's close or convenient. With technology and property-management companies, you can own and manage investments in markets across the country that offer better returns.

Myth 5: "You Need to Be Smart."

Reality: Real estate investing isn't rocket science. You don't need a genius IQ; persistence, logical thinking, and a reasonable approach are more than enough. The math involved is simple—basic addition, subtraction, and percentages—and tools such as spreadsheets or software make it even easier.

Myth 6: "You Need to Have Business Experience."

Reality: Everyone starts somewhere, and real estate is one of the simplest and lowest-risk businesses to begin with minimal experience. It's also one of the most affordable businesses to enter, with options like low down payments or creative financing strategies to reduce capital requirements. Through real estate, you can gain valuable experience while building wealth.

Myth 7: "You Have to Manage Properties Yourself."

Reality: Many people hesitate to invest because they don't want to deal with tenants, toilets, and trash. But property-management companies can handle day-to-day operations for you, making real estate investing much more hands-off than most people think.

Myth 8: "You Need to Wait for the Perfect Market Timing."

Reality: There is no such thing as perfect timing in real estate. The best time to invest is when you find a deal that makes financial sense. Trying to predict the market can lead to missed opportunities; wealth is built by being in the market, not by waiting on the sidelines.

By addressing these myths, it becomes clear that real estate is accessible, achievable, and rewarding for anyone willing to take action. The biggest obstacle is not external—it's overcoming the misconceptions that hold you back. Start where you are, use what you have, and let your journey begin.

CHAPTER 8: HOW TO FINANCE REAL ESTATE

Debt is not a tool; it is a method to make banks wealthy, not you.

— DAVE RAMSEY

This quote is something I imagine Robert Kiyosaki, Grant Cardone, and many others who have successfully used leverage in real estate would not say. They've shown that strategic use of debt in real estate can be a powerful wealth-building tool. Leverage enables you to control high-value assets with minimal up-front capital, potentially multiplying your returns. However, it's crucial to acknowledge the risks. Over-leveraging, especially during market downturns, can lead to financial losses and missed opportunities. The key lies in understanding how to use leverage responsibly to maximize rewards while minimizing risk.

Financing real estate is one of the most powerful wealth-building strategies available, thanks to the unique advantage of leverage. Unlike most asset classes, real estate allows investors to purchase a large income-producing asset with a relatively small up-front investment. This ability to borrow money to acquire appreciating assets is unparalleled in other investments, such as stocks or bonds. However, leverage comes with its own set of risks, especially during market downturns. Mismanaging debt or becoming over-leveraged can quickly turn a promising investment into a financial liability.

In this chapter, we'll explore the financing options available for real estate, focusing on single-family homes and small multifamily properties (four units or fewer). We'll also cover financing basics, qualifications, and unconventional methods that can help you build your real estate portfolio while mitigating risks.

The Power and Risks of Leverage

Leverage, in real estate, refers to using borrowed capital—typically in the form of a mortgage—to acquire property. This allows investors to control a large asset with a relatively small up-front investment, maximizing potential returns.

Take John and Mark, for example. Both wanted to invest in real estate, but they took different approaches. John saved for years, determined to buy a rental property in cash. By the time he had enough, property prices had risen and he could only afford a small condo that barely generated any cash flow. Meanwhile, Mark used leverage—he put down 20 percent on a duplex early on, allowing him to start earning rental income while benefiting from appreciation. A few years later, Mark refinanced and used that equity to buy another property, exponentially growing his portfolio. While John was still saving, Mark had already built a real estate business.

Leverage amplifies your returns in real estate by allowing you to control a large asset with a small amount of your own money. For instance, with a 20 percent down payment, you can acquire a property worth five times that amount, enabling you to benefit from appreciation, rental income, and tax advantages on the full property value—not just on the portion you paid for.

However, leverage is a double-edged sword. In a rising market, it magnifies gains, but in a declining market, it can amplify losses. Over-leveraging—borrowing too much relative to your income and property's cash flow—can lead to financial strain. If property values drop, or if rents fall below expectations, highly leveraged investors may struggle to cover their debt obligations, risking foreclosure or forced property sales.

The key is to strike a balance: use leverage to grow your portfolio, but always maintain enough cash flow and reserves to weather market fluctuations.

Financing Options for Real Estate

There are many financing options available in real estate, each suited for different types of properties and investment strategies. In general, financing falls into two main categories: residential financing and commercial financing. Residential financing applies to single-family homes and small multifamily properties with one to four units, making it the most common option for individual investors and homebuyers. These loans typically offer lower interest rates and longer repayment terms (such as 15- or 30-year mortgages), and are often backed by government programs like FHA, VA, or conventional loan products. Conversely, commercial financing provides funding for properties with five or more units, including office buildings, retail centers, and other income-producing properties. Commercial loans generally have shorter terms, higher interest rates, and stricter qualification requirements, with lenders focusing on the property's income potential rather than just the borrower's personal creditworthiness. Understanding the distinctions between these financing types is crucial for selecting the right loan product for your investment goals.

Residential Financing

Residential financing targets single-family homes and small multifamily properties (1–4 units) and is typically easier to qualify for than commercial loans. These loans offer longer repayment terms, lower interest rates, and flexible down-payment options. The most common types include conventional, FHA, VA, and USDA loans, each catering to different borrower needs. Since this

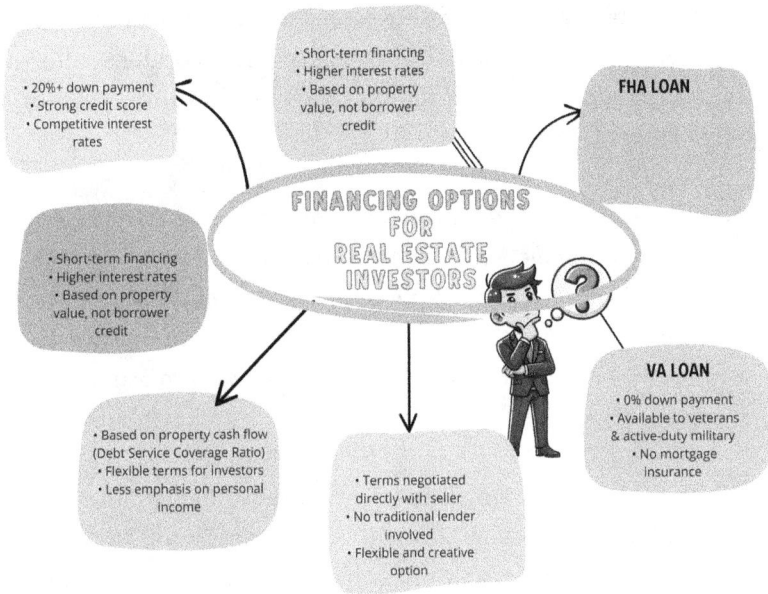

book is called *Mastering Single-Family Real Estate*, we will focus only on residential financing, as it is the primary method used to finance single-family homes. Understanding these loan options is essential for building a strong foundation in real estate investing.

FHA Loans: A Pathway to Homeownership

FHA loans make homeownership more accessible by offering low down payments (as little as 3.5 percent) and flexible credit requirements. Unlike conventional loans, they also allow higher debt-to-income ratios, making it easier for buyers to qualify. However, FHA loans come with mortgage insurance premiums (MIP), which add to overall costs unless refinanced into a conventional loan later. Loan limits vary by location, with higher caps in expensive markets. Additionally, FHA loans require a property appraisal to ensure that the home meets safety and livability standards.

Many people assume FHA loans are only for first-time buyers, but they can also be a great tool for investors. Since they can finance 2–4 unit properties, FHA loans make house hacking an option—allowing buyers to live in one unit and rent out the others to cover most or all of the mortgage.

Take John, for example. He used an FHA loan to buy a duplex. He lived in one unit and rented the other. The rental income covered 70 percent of his mortgage, making homeownership more affordable while building equity. A few years later, he refinanced into a conventional loan, removed the mortgage insurance, and used his FHA eligibility again to buy another property.

While FHA loans are mainly for primary residences, they can be an excellent stepping stone into real estate investing. Borrowers can only have one FHA loan at a time, meaning they must refinance or pay it off before using another. However, for those starting out, this is one of the best ways to buy property with little money down while generating rental income and building long-term wealth.

VA Loans: A Powerful Option for Veterans and Service Members

VA loans, backed by the U.S. Department of Veterans Affairs, make homeownership more affordable for eligible veterans, active-duty service members, and certain National Guard or Reserve members. With no down payment, no private mortgage insurance (PMI), and competitive interest rates, VA loans offer some of the best financing terms available. They also have flexible credit requirements, and as of 2020, veterans with full entitlement have no loan limits, meaning they can borrow as much as their lender approves.

To qualify, veterans need a Certificate of Eligibility (COE) based on their service history, such as 90 days of active duty during wartime or 181 days during peacetime. The VA offers extra perks with their loans, such as lower closing costs, assumable loans, no prepayment penalties, and a one-time funding fee—which can be waived for those with service-connected disabilities. Borrowers can use VA loans for primary residences, including single-family homes, VA-approved condos, and even multiunit properties—making them a powerful wealth-building tool.

Beyond the initial purchase, VA loans offer refinancing options, like the Interest Rate Reduction Refinance Loan (IRRRL), to secure lower interest rates or a cash-out refinance to tap into home equity. While VA loans require property appraisals to meet safety and livability standards, they remain one of the most powerful financing options available. With no down payment and long-term affordability, VA loans give veterans a unique advantage in homeownership and real estate investing.

USDA Loans: No-Money-Down Rural Homeownership

USDA loans, backed by the U.S. Department of Agriculture, make buying a home easier for low- to moderate-income families in rural and suburban areas. With 100 percent financing (no down payment), lower mortgage insurance costs, and competitive interest rates, they offer one of the most affordable paths to homeownership. Borrowers can qualify with flexible credit requirements, often with scores as low as 640. Mortgage insurance costs are also lower than FHA loans, with a 1 percent up-front guarantee fee (which can be rolled into the loan) and a 0.35 percent annual fee.

To qualify, the home must be in a USDA-designated rural or suburban area, and household income cannot exceed 115 percent of the area's median income. USDA loans are for primary residences only and require homes to meet safety and livability standards. They also come in two types: the Guaranteed Loan for moderate-income borrowers and the Direct Loan for very-low-income buyers.

USDA loans also offer streamlined refinancing options to secure lower rates with minimal hassle. Compared to FHA or conventional loans, they provide greater affordability and flexibility, making them a powerful tool for families to build wealth through homeownership —without the burden of a large down payment.

Conventional Loans: A Flexible Path to Wealth

Conventional loans are one of the most versatile financing options, offering competitive terms for buyers with strong credit and stable finances. Unlike FHA, VA, or USDA loans, they aren't government-backed, meaning lenders take on more risk—but this also means greater flexibility for borrowers. One major advantage is the ability to remove private mortgage insurance (PMI) once 20 percent equity is reached, reducing long-term costs. Down payments range from 3 percent for first-time buyers to 5–20 percent for others, with larger down payments leading to better rates and no PMI.

There are two main types: conforming loans, which follow Fannie Mae and Freddie Mac limits ($726,200 in most areas, up to $1,089,300 in high-cost regions), and non-conforming loans, like jumbo loans, which exceed these limits. Borrowers typically need a 620+ credit score and a manageable debt-to-income (DTI) ratio of 36–45 percent. While these loans require solid documentation, they also offer customizable terms, no up-front mortgage insurance, and the flexibility to finance second homes or investment properties.

Though conventional loans have stricter qualifications, they provide long-term affordability and wealth-building potential. Buyers can use gift funds for down payments, negotiate seller-paid closing costs, and refinance to access home equity. Whether you're purchasing, investing, or refinancing, conventional loans offer the freedom and cost-efficiency to grow your wealth.

DSCR Loans: The Investor's Secret Weapon

DSCR (Debt Service Coverage Ratio) loans focus on the property's income, not on your personal paycheck. Unlike traditional loans, lenders don't look at your job income or tax returns. Instead, they see if the property earns enough rent to cover its mortgage. A DSCR of

1.25 or higher means the property makes at least 25 percent more than it costs to own, making it a self-sustaining investment.

The best part is that DSCR loans don't count against your personal debt-to-income (DTI) ratio, so you can keep borrowing without hitting limits. Investors can take out multiple DSCR loans, making them a powerful tool for building a real estate portfolio. Down payments typically range from 20–25 percent, allowing investors to use the property's cash flow to grow faster.

While DSCR loans may have slightly higher interest rates, their flexibility and scalability make them a top choice for serious investors. With no cap on the number of loans and a focus on property income, DSCR loans are the fast track to financial freedom, whether you're buying single-family rentals, multifamily units, or commercial properties.

Unconventional Financing Methods

Not every real estate deal fits into a traditional loan box. Some of the best investors think outside the bank and use creative financing to acquire properties with little money down or even no credit check. *Imagine Sarah, a new investor who couldn't qualify for a mortgage. Instead of giving up, she worked out a seller financing deal in which the owner let her make payments directly—no bank involved.* Others use lease options, private lenders, or hard-money loans to fund deals quickly. These unconventional methods give investors more flexibility, faster approvals, and the ability to buy properties others can't. The key is knowing your options and using the right strategy at the right time.

Loan Assumption: The Shortcut to a Better Deal

Imagine two buyers—Jake and Lisa—both wanting the same house. Jake gets a brand-new mortgage at 7 percent interest, paying high closing costs and starting at the beginning of a 30-year loan, where most of his payment goes toward interest rather than toward the house. Lisa, on the other hand, finds out the seller has an assumable FHA loan at 3 percent interest with ten years already paid off. Instead of taking out a new loan, she takes over the seller's mortgage at the original low rate, skipping most lender fees and stepping into a loan in which more of her payment now goes toward building equity—not just paying interest.

This is the power of loan assumption. Buyers inherit a seasoned mortgage, meaning they start where the seller left off—closer to paying off the home instead of resetting the clock on a thirty-year loan. This is especially valuable when interest rates are high, allowing buyers to secure a rate from years ago, saving thousands of dollars over time. Since the loan is already in place, the process can also move faster with fewer out-of-pocket costs.

To assume a loan, the buyer still needs lender approval, just as with a traditional mortgage, proving they can afford the payments. However, instead of applying for a new loan, the lender transfers the existing mortgage into the buyer's name, keeping the same low interest rate and repayment terms. The only catch is that if the seller has built up a lot of equity, the buyer must cover the difference between the remaining loan balance and the purchase price—either with cash, a second loan, or a seller-financed agreement.

For investors and homebuyers alike, loan assumption is a hidden shortcut to securing lower rates, faster equity growth, and a smarter way to buy real estate—especially when borrowing costs are high.

Seller Financing: A Flexible Alternative to Traditional Mortgages

Seller financing offers a creative and flexible solution for buyers and sellers, bypassing banks and allowing the buyer to make payments directly to the seller. In this arrangement, the seller acts as the lender, using their equity in the property to finance the purchase. This means that the seller holds the mortgage and the buyer makes agreed-upon payments over time, just as they would with a traditional bank loan.

The best-case scenario for seller financing is when the property is free and clear, meaning there's no existing mortgage on it. Since no bank is involved, the process is often faster and with lower costs, as there are no loan origination fees or other standard lender charges. Buyers who may struggle with traditional mortgage approval because of credit issues or irregular income can benefit from this arrangement, as the terms—including interest rate, down payment, and repayment schedule—are negotiable.

For sellers, this approach can make it easier to sell a property, particularly if it's been sitting on the market for a while. It also provides an opportunity to generate a steady stream of income, as they receive regular payments with interest over time. Additionally, structuring the sale as installment payments can offer tax advantages, spreading capital gains taxation over several years instead of taking a large tax hit all at once.

A seller-financed deal is typically structured with a promissory note and a deed of trust, formalizing the agreement and protecting both parties. Some agreements may include a balloon payment, in which the buyer makes smaller monthly payments but must pay off the remaining balance in a lump sum at the end of the term.

While seller financing is a powerful tool, it comes with risks. Buyers should verify the property's title to ensure that there are no undisclosed issues. Sellers should carefully vet the buyer's financial ability to make payments and may want to work with a real estate attorney to ensure that all legal documentation is airtight.

When done correctly, seller financing can be a win-win strategy, making homeownership accessible for buyers and offering sellers a reliable income stream without the complexities of a traditional bank loan.

A Tale of Two Sellers

Let's talk about two sellers—Mike and Tom.

Mike owned a rental property free and clear, but the market was slow and buyers weren't biting. Instead of waiting, he decided to offer seller financing. Within weeks, he found a motivated buyer who couldn't qualify for a traditional mortgage but had a solid income and a reasonable down payment. Mike sold the house at full asking price, charged an 8-percent interest rate, and structured the loan over fifteen years. Now every month he collects payments, just like a bank, and over time he'll make tens of thousands of dollars in interest alone—on top of his sale price.

Tom had a similar house on the market, but insisted on waiting for a traditional buyer. Months passed. He cut the price twice to attract interest. He still had to pay property taxes, maintenance costs, and insurance while the house sat vacant. Selling nearly a year later, he had to accept a lower offer, resulting in a loss on carrying costs.

Mike didn't just sell his house faster, but he also turned it into a long-term income stream. He became the bank, earning passive income without managing tenants or dealing with vacancies. As for Tom, he just walked away with less than he wanted.

The choice is obvious. Seller financing isn't just about selling a house; it's about turning a sale into an investment.

Wraparound Mortgages: How Sellers Can Profit While Still Owing the Bank

A wraparound mortgage is a way for a seller to help a buyer finance a home even if the seller still has a mortgage on it. Think of it like this: The seller still owes money to the bank, but instead of the buyer getting a new loan from another bank, the buyer pays the seller every month, and the seller uses part of that money to keep paying his own mortgage. The seller charges a higher interest rate than what he pays the bank, so he makes extra money on the difference. It's like borrowing a friend's bike and charging someone else to rent it— while still making payments on it yourself.

However, this type of financing comes with risks. If the seller cannot pay his original mortgage, the bank could foreclose on the property, even if the buyer has been making payments. That's why it's crucial to consult a real estate attorney before doing a wraparound mortgage. An attorney can draft a proper contract and ensure that the deal follows state and federal laws, protecting both the buyer and seller from unexpected problems.

Subject-To Financing: A Creative Path to Property Ownership

Subject-to financing is a powerful real estate strategy in which the buyer takes over payments on the seller's existing mortgage without formally assuming the loan. While the mortgage remains in the seller's name, the buyer gains ownership of the property, making this approach especially attractive for those looking to enter the market with minimal up-front capital. By utilizing the seller's existing loan terms, buyers can often secure lower interest rates than those currently offered, making subject-to financing a cost-effective and creative solution for acquiring property.

However, subject-to financing carries inherent risks. The most significant is the due-on-sale clause, which allows the lender to demand full repayment if they discover the transfer of ownership. Success in these deals hinges on clear, well-drafted legal agreements and a high degree of trust between the buyer and seller. Despite these challenges, subject-to financing remains a valuable tool for investors who understand the nuances of the process.

My First Subject-To Deal: Houston Beginnings: My first subject-to deal marked my entry into real estate investment. Living in Los Angeles as a real estate agent and travel nurse, I visited Houston with my fiancée to spend time with her family. During a conversation, my future mother-in-law mentioned that she wanted to sell her rental property to escape the headaches of being a landlord. Recognizing an opportunity, I proposed a subject-to deal that would allow me to take over her existing mortgage. This arrangement required minimal cash up front and enabled me to benefit from her low-interest loan. This first property not only helped me build equity with limited capital, but also set the foundation for my real estate journey, showcasing the potential of subject-to financing for savvy investors.

The Opportunity: Initially, I offered to help my mother-in-law manage the rental more easily by providing advice and strategies. However, she was adamant about getting rid of it entirely. The property was valued at $190,000 based on comparable sales in the area. If she had sold it traditionally, she would have incurred significant costs:

- Realtor fees (6 percent): $11,400
- Seller closing costs (2 percent): $3,800

After accounting for her $100,000 mortgage balance, she would net approximately $74,800.

My Proposal: Instead of selling traditionally, I offered her a subject-to deal:

- •Purchase price: $200,000
- She would avoid realtor fees and closing costs.
- I would take title through an LLC while keeping her existing loan in place.
- I drafted a contract to ensure legal clarity and trust.

With this arrangement, she netted about $100,000, significantly more than her original plan, and relieved herself of landlord responsibilities. I found a way to help her benefit more than she would have by simply selling through an agent.

Financing Details

- Down payment: $100,000 (split into $50,000 up front and $50,000 over three years)
- Mortgage payments: I continued paying her existing loan.
- Amortization benefit: Since her loan was in its seventh year, more of my payments went toward principal rather than interest.

The Outcome: This deal became my first rental property. Since I had already used my FHA loan for a home in Riverview, Florida, and my credit was not ideal, subject-to financing was perfect. Here's what I achieved:

- Cash flow: The property generated rental income.
- Education: Managing a rental taught me invaluable lessons beyond theory.
- Airbnb experiment: I even leveraged the property for short-term rentals before converting it back to a long-term rental.
- Appreciation: Eventually, I sold the property for $240,000, earning a substantial profit.

Risk Management—Addressing the Due-on-Sale Clause: One of the primary concerns with subject-to financing is the due-on-sale clause, which allows lenders to demand full repayment of the loan if the property ownership changes. When I first encountered this strategy, a mentor explained that while the clause exists, it is rarely enforced. Lenders are generally more interested in receiving timely payments than triggering a lengthy and costly process of enforcing the clause. Even if triggered, the process involves back-and-forth communication, often giving buyers enough time to negotiate a refinance or resolve the situation.

That said, every case is unique, and lenders' actions can vary. What worked for me may not apply universally. For anyone considering subject-to financing, it's crucial to consult with a knowledgeable real estate attorney to fully understand the risks and ensure that proper legal safeguards are in place. Taking this step can help you navigate the process with confidence and protect your investment from unforeseen complications.

Final Thoughts on Subject-To Financing: Subject-to financing is a powerful tool for real estate investors, especially those with limited capital or credit. By structuring creative deals, you can acquire properties, generate cash flow, and build wealth. However, always ensure proper legal agreements and clear communication to mitigate risks.

This strategy jump-started my real estate journey and provided a foundation for future investments. If you're considering subject-to financing, remember that every deal is an opportunity to learn and grow.

Key Takeaways

Real estate financing offers a wide range of options, from traditional loans like FHA and conventional mortgages to creative strategies such as seller financing and subject-to deals. The best choice depends on your financial situation, investment goals, and market conditions. Each financing method comes with its own advantages and risks, making it essential to weigh the power of leverage against potential downsides.

No matter which strategy you choose, the key to successful investing lies in understanding loan terms, repayment structures, and cash-flow potential. Always ensure that your investment generates positive cash flow, even after factoring in financing costs. With the right preparation and informed decision-making, you can use financing as a powerful tool to build a profitable and resilient real estate portfolio.

CHAPTER 9: THE MATH OF REAL ESTATE: WHAT MAKES A DEAL WORK

With real estate, understanding the math is the cornerstone of making smart investment decisions. Numbers don't lie, and your ability to analyze them will determine whether a deal sinks or soars. In this chapter, we'll break down the essential concepts, such as cash flow, after repair value (ARV), and how the math varies between flipping and buy-and-hold strategies. We'll also dive into key profitability factors like inflation, holding costs, and capital expenditures (CapEx). Lastly, we'll explore the powerful tool of cash-out refinancing and how it can help you build wealth by reinvesting tax-free capital.

Cash Flow: The Lifeblood of Buy-and-Hold Investments

Cash flow is the net income you earn from a rental property after accounting for all expenses. It's the measure of whether a property is making you money month after month or draining your wallet. The formula is simple:

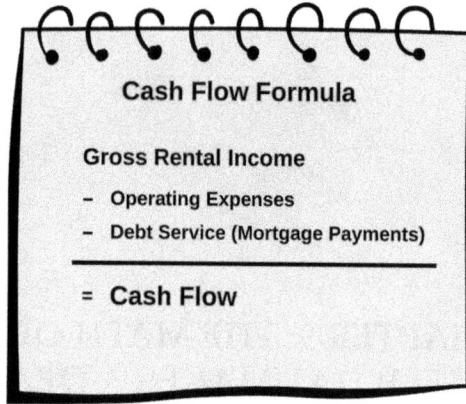

Cash Flow Formula

Gross Rental Income
- Operating Expenses
- Debt Service (Mortgage Payments)

= **Cash Flow**

The Formula for Cash Flow

Operating expenses include property-management fees, insurance, taxes, repairs, and any utilities you cover as the landlord. Positive cash flow means you're making money, while negative cash flow could spell trouble unless you have a clear plan to turn things around.

A TALE of Two Investors

Consider Dave and Mark, two investors who bought similar rental properties in the same neighborhood.

Dave ran his numbers carefully. His rental property brought in $2,000 a month in rent. After paying for the mortgage, property taxes, insurance, maintenance, and management fees, his total expenses came to $1,600. That left him with a positive cash flow of $400 per month—or $4,800 per year in passive income. Over time, that steady income helped him reinvest in more properties, growing his portfolio without stress.

Mark, on the other hand, jumped into a deal without crunching the numbers. His mortgage and expenses ended up being higher than his rental income, leaving him with a negative cash flow of $200 per month. To cover *the shortfall, he had to dip into his savings. Eventually, when an unexpected repair hit, he was forced to sell the property at a loss.*

The difference? Cash-flow discipline. In real estate, the numbers don't lie. A property that pays you every month can build wealth, while one that drains your bank account can become a financial headache.

After Repair Value (ARV): The Key to Flipping

Flipping properties is a numbers game. Success hinges on your ability to accurately estimate the ARV—the property's market value after all renovations are complete. To calculate ARV, you must analyze comparable sales (comps) in the area. These are recently sold properties that are similar in size, condition, and location.

The formula looks like this:

ARV = Purchase Price + Value of Renovations

For instance, if you purchase a fixer-upper for $150,000 and spend $50,000 on renovations, your target ARV might be $250,000, assuming the comps support that value. The math doesn't stop there, though. To determine if a flip is worth pursuing, investors often rely on the 70-Percent Rule:

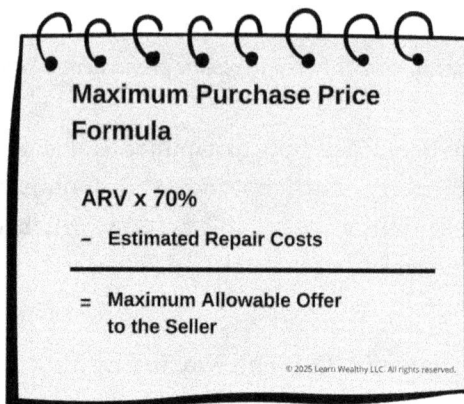

Maximum Purchase Price Formula

ARV x 70%
- Estimated Repair Costs
_____

= Maximum Allowable Offer
to the Seller

The Maximum Price You Can Offer the Seller

Maximum Purchase Price = (ARV × 70%) – Estimated Repair Costs

If the ARV is $250,000 and repairs cost $50,000, the most you should pay for the property is $125,000 to ensure a profitable flip.

A great way to sharpen your investing skills is to practice running the numbers. Try finding a property in your area and calculate its After Repair Value (ARV)—how much it would be worth after fixing it up. Then figure out the maximum price you should pay to make a good profit. It's like playing a real estate treasure hunt in which the prize is a great deal and a smart investment!

Flipping vs. Buy-and-Hold: Two Paths, Two Payoffs

Flipping is all about the quick win—buying a property, fixing it up, and selling it fast for a profit. The key number here is the profit margin, which comes from the After Repair Value (ARV) minus all costs (purchase price, renovation, holding costs, and selling fees). The faster you flip, the more you keep.

Buy-and-hold, on the other hand, is a long-term wealth builder. Here the focus is on cash flow and equity growth. Your rental income covers the mortgage and expenses, and over time, the property appreciates, adding to your net worth. It's like planting a tree that keeps growing and producing fruit year after year.

Both strategies have their place; flipping is great for fast cash, while buy-and-hold creates lasting wealth. The best choice? The one that fits your financial goals and risk tolerance.

HOLDING COSTS: **The Silent Profit Killer**

Holding costs are the expenses you incur while owning a property, but before it starts generating income. These costs include property taxes, utilities, insurance, and loan interest. For flippers, minimizing holding costs is crucial because every month a property sits unsold eats into profit. For buy-and-hold investors, these costs are part of the long-term expense structure and must be factored into cash-flow analysis.

Jake was an ambitious house flipper who found what he thought was the perfect deal—a run-down house in a hot market. He planned to renovate it in three months and sell for a big payday. But things didn't go as planned. First, permits got delayed. Then his contractor missed deadlines. Before he knew it, six months had passed and the house still wasn't ready for sale. Meanwhile, his holding costs kept stacking up—loan payments, property taxes, insurance, and utilities drained more than $1,000 per month from his budget. By the time the house finally hit the market, interest rates had ticked up, buyers had more options, and he had to slash his asking price to sell. Instead of walking away with a hefty profit, Jake barely broke even— all because he underestimated holding costs.

The lesson? Time is money. The longer you hold a property without income, the more it eats into your bottom line. Whether flipping or buying to hold, always factor in holding costs—because they don't just take up time; they also take up profit.

Repairs and CapEx: Plan for the Unexpected

Owning rental property isn't just about collecting rent; it's also about being prepared for what will eventually break. Regular repairs, like fixing a leaky faucet or replacing a broken window, are part of the job. But then there are the big ones—capital expenditures (CapEx)—the major, infrequent costs that can wipe out months of profit in an instant. A new roof, a failing HVAC system, or major plumbing issues aren't just costly—they're inevitable.

Ashley was excited about her first rental property. She ran the numbers, saw a solid $300 per month in cash flow, and felt confident that she had made a brilliant investment. Every month, that extra $3,600 per year felt like a win—until reality hit.

After four years of collecting rent, Ashley got a call from her tenant. The roof was leaking. She hoped it would be a minor repair, but the inspection told a different story. The entire roof needed replacing—a $14,000 job. Suddenly, Ashley realized she had made a critical mistake. She had never set aside money for capital expenditures, assuming she could just pocket the rental income. Worse, she had no cash reserves, meaning she had no easy way to cover the cost.

All the cash flow she had earned over the past four years was gone in an instant. With no other options, she had to take out a high-interest loan just to make the repair. What once felt like a wealth-building investment now felt like a financial trap.

If Ashley had planned ahead, setting aside 10–15 percent of her rental income for repairs and CapEx, she could have covered the cost without stress. But like many first-time investors, she learned the hard way. Real estate isn't just about making money; it's about keeping it.

The Power of Cash-Out Refinancing

Cash-Out Refinancing—Unlocking Wealth Without Selling: Cash-out refinancing is one of the most powerful tools in real estate. Imagine being able to pull cash out of your property's equity without selling it—and doing so tax-free. This strategy allows you to tap into the value your home has gained over time and reinvest it to grow your wealth even faster.

I remember using this exact strategy with my very first primary residence. I bought the home for $200,000, putting down 20 percent ($40,000) and financing the rest with a mortgage. Over the years, the home appreciated to $300,000, while my mortgage balance shrunk to $150,000 as I made regular payments. Instead of selling and losing a great asset, I refinanced it at 75 percent of its new value, securing a new loan of $225,000. After paying off the remaining mortgage, I walked away with $75,000 in cash—completely tax-free.

That money became the seed for my next investment. I used it to buy a rental property, which started generating monthly cash flow while my original home kept appreciating. I was still the owner, still building equity, and now I had another income-producing asset in my portfolio.

The best part? I didn't have to sell anything to make it happen. This is how real estate investors turn one property into many—by using the wealth locked in their homes to keep their money working for them.

Key Takeaways

Real estate isn't just about buying houses; it's also about making the numbers work. Whether you're holding a rental for long-term cash flow or flipping a property for a quick profit, knowing your math is what separates smart investors from those who lose money. Every deal comes down to key factors: cash flow, renovation costs, holding costs, and CapEx. If you don't account for these, even a great-looking deal can turn into a financial nightmare.

The good news? When you understand how to use numbers to your advantage, real estate can be a wealth-building machine. Tools like cash-out refinancing allow you to pull equity from a property and reinvest it—without selling. That means you can buy one property, then use it to buy another, and another, growing your portfolio without draining your bank account.

At the end of the day, real estate isn't just about buildings, but it's also about the math behind the deals. Learn the numbers and make them work for you, and you'll be on your way to financial freedom.

CHAPTER 10: BUILDING YOUR TEAM AS A REAL ESTATE INVESTOR

R eal estate investing isn't a solo venture. Behind every successful investor is a solid team of professionals who help navigate the complex world of property transactions, financing, and property management. In this chapter, we'll explore the essential team members you need, how to find them, and tips for building long-lasting, productive relationships.

Alone we can do so little; together we can do so much.

— HELEN KELLER

Why You Need a Team

The real estate world is vast, with every deal involving multiple moving parts. Having the right team allows you to leverage expertise by tapping into specialized knowledge in areas such as legal compliance, market analysis, and property management. It saves you time by letting professionals handle critical tasks, freeing you up to focus on finding and analyzing deals. A strong team also reduces risk by helping you avoid costly mistakes and ensuring that you make informed decisions. Most importantly, it enables you to scale your business, allowing you to take on more deals and grow your portfolio faster.

To build a successful real estate business, you need the right people in your corner. Let's look at the key team members who will help you navigate the complexities of real estate investing.

Real Estate Agent

A real estate agent is your boots on the ground, providing market insights, access to deals, and guidance during transactions. The right agent isn't just someone who helps you buy or sell a house; they should also understand investment strategies, cash flow, cap rates, and off-market opportunities. An agent who specializes in working with investors can be the key to finding and securing profitable deals.

Real-Life Example:

My friend, who is also my real estate agent in Florida, helped my mom purchase an investment property. He was the same agent who helped me buy my very first home as a primary residence in Riverview, Florida, near Tampa. Even as a licensed real estate agent myself, I was never licensed in Florida, so I still needed an agent when buying in that market. Years later, when my mom had money to invest, our agent came across a fantastic off-market deal—a one-acre property for only $37,000, and it already had a mobile home on it that could be rented out. My mom paid for it in cash and is now cash-flowing on that property. The best part? Only a small portion of the land is currently being used. Now my mom and I are discussing part-nering up to develop the rest of the property to maximize its cash-flow potential. And of course, our trusted agent in Tampa will be instrumental in making this happen, especially since I can't be in Florida all the time while my kids are in Texas.

Finding a great real estate agent takes some effort, but it's worth it.

Attending local real estate meetups is a great way to network and find agents who work closely with investors. Asking for referrals from other successful investors can also lead you to experienced professionals who understand the game. Searching online for agents specializing in investment properties can help, but always vet them thoroughly; make sure they truly understand cash flow, rental markets, and investor-friendly strategies. A strong agent can help you scale your portfolio faster by consistently bringing you profitable opportunities.

Property Manager

A property manager handles tenant issues, maintenance, and rent collection, ensuring that your investment runs smoothly. A property manager is crucial if you own multiple properties or live far from your investments.

Real-Life Example:

My friend Mike had major headaches with his rental property because his real estate agent, who was also acting as his property manager, wasn't handling a serious issue. His tenant was parking a huge taco truck in the driveway, violating HOA rules. Mike kept getting fined, but his so-called property manager wasn't doing anything about it. I told Mike he needed to replace that agent with an actual professional property-management company—one that had the experience and resources to handle these kinds of issues properly. Mike took my advice, switched to a professional management company, and they immediately resolved the issue, saving him from ongoing HOA fines and frustration.

Because of that experience, when Mike bought his next property, he partnered with me. We co-invested in a single-family buy-and-hold rental, and this time we made sure to hire an experienced property-management company from the start. Since I was a licensed real estate agent, I negotiated directly with the seller and structured the deal in a way that saved the seller 6 percent in realtor commissions. Because the seller didn't have to pay an agent, he was more willing to work with us on the price, which allowed us to secure a great deal on the property. To this day, we still own that rental together, and we have zero to little headache with it. We're not involved in the day-to-day operations at all, which frees us up to focus on other investments—a true definition of passive income.

One big lesson from Mike's situation is that a real estate agent's primary role is buying and selling houses, not managing rental properties. Many agents take on property management as a side gig, but their priorities are often focused on closing deals, which can create a conflict of interest. They might not have the time, experience, or dedication to handle tenant issues, maintenance problems, and lease enforcement properly. This is why, when you build your real estate team, every member should be an expert in their specific role—more proficient at it than you are. Whether it's a property manager, contractor, lender, or attorney, you want professionals who specialize in their field, not someone trying to juggle multiple roles.

Finding the right property manager takes some effort, but it's worth it. It's important to interview several property-management companies to compare their services, experience, and responsiveness. Reading online reviews and checking references from other investors can also provide valuable insight into their track record. Before committing long-term, it's smart to start with a trial period to see how they handle tenant issues, maintenance requests, and overall property management. A great property manager can mean the difference between a smooth, passive income stream and a never-ending list of problems.

Lender or Mortgage Broker

Financing is the backbone of real estate investing, and a good lender or mortgage broker can make all the difference in securing the right loan for your strategy, whether it's a conventional loan, an FHA loan, or hard-money financing. I've seen investors run into serious issues by working with lenders who don't understand real estate investing.

One investor found a fantastic rental property at a great price, but their loan officer kept delaying the process, asking for unnecessary documents, and ultimately couldn't get the deal closed on time. Because of the delay, they lost out on a cash-flowing property well below market value. Frustrated, they switched to an investor-friendly mortgage broker who not only understood the urgency of locking in deals, but also had access to lenders who catered specifically to real estate investors. When they found their next deal, the mortgage broker got everything processed quickly, secured better terms, and closed on time—allowing them to secure a property that's still making money for them today. Finding the right mortgage broker or lender takes some research, but it's worth it. Networking at real estate investment groups, researching both local and national lenders, and comparing loan terms, interest rates, and responsiveness can help ensure that you have someone on your team who won't let financing issues stand in the way of a great deal.

Contractor or Maintenance Person

A reliable contractor can turn a fixer-upper into a profitable property, while a maintenance person or a handyman can handle day-to-day maintenance. Both are critical to maintaining and improving your investments.

Real-Life Example:

When I was still a travel nurse and real estate agent in California, and when the Airbnb market was booming, I converted two of my single-family rentals in Houston, Texas, into short-term rentals, listing them on Airbnb and VRBO. At first, I hired a handyman through an app called TaskRabbit for minor jobs like fixing chipped furniture or patching walls. One day, while visiting one of my properties in Houston, I met the handyman in person while he was working. We exchanged numbers, and from then on, he became my go-to guy for maintenance and repairs. Over time, he handled everything from quick fixes to larger renovations, keeping my properties in top shape for short-term guests. Since my single-family rentals are long-term rentals again and are now managed by a professional property-management company that has its own maintenance team, he now mainly works on my primary home and for friends I've referred him to. Having a trustworthy contractor or handy-person in your corner can make property management significantly easier and ensure that your investments remain in great condition.

Finding the right contractor takes time, but it's essential. Asking for recommendations from other investors or property managers can lead to reliable professionals. Testing them first with small projects helps gauge their skill and reliability. It's also important to verify their licenses, insurance, and past work to make sure they're experienced and qualified. The right contractor can save you money, time, and countless headaches in the long run.

CPA (Certified Public Accountant)

CPAs with real estate experience will help you minimize taxes, ensure compliance, and maximize deductions. They're vital for keeping your finances in order and planning your investment strategy.

Real-Life Example:

The taxes for my LLCs, where I hold my properties, as well as my personal taxes, are managed by a professional accounting firm. I don't use regular tax preparers because I'm running a legitimate business. Real estate is the asset class with the most tax advantages, and I need to maximize every opportunity available. Every year, I file taxes for my LLCs first, and those LLCs often generate paper losses even though they actually hold cash-flowing real estate. A month later, when I file my personal taxes, those losses carry over, reducing my overall tax burden. I only know the basics when it comes to tax loopholes, but the tax code is massive, and having a professional who understands it inside and out is a game changer. My CPA helps me navigate complex tax strategies, ensuring that I take full advantage of deductions and incentives that I otherwise wouldn't have even known existed. This level of expertise is an invaluable asset that directly impacts my bottom line.

Finding the right CPA means working with someone who specializes in real estate and understands how to structure investments for tax efficiency. A skilled CPA doesn't just prepare returns, but they also help you plan ahead, optimize deductions, and keep more of your hard-earned money. Having a professional on your side isn't just beneficial, but it's also a crazy advantage.

Real Estate Attorney

A real estate attorney ensures that your contracts are airtight and protects you from legal pitfalls. They are particularly useful for complex transactions, landlord-tenant disputes, or structuring LLCs for your properties. While I don't need an attorney for every aspect of my real estate business, their expertise is invaluable when it comes to planning and strategy. Over time, I've learned to set up my own LLCs, draft my own deeds to transfer properties between my personal name and my LLCs, and handle basic legal paperwork. However, where I truly rely on my attorney is for the bigger picture—understanding why an LLC makes sense for one property but a trust might be a better option for another, especially for anonymity and asset protection.

Additionally, whenever I partner with someone on an investment property, I have my attorney draft the operating agreement. This ensures that ownership stakes, financial obligations, and responsibilities are clearly spelled out, preventing any confusion or disputes down the road. A good real estate attorney isn't just someone who reacts to problems, but they also help you proactively structure your investments in a way that protects you and sets you up for long-term success.

Insurance Agent

An insurance agent is essential for safeguarding your investments, ensuring that your properties are protected from unexpected disasters, liability issues, and tenant-related risks. A landlord who skips proper insurance coverage to save money might not realize the mistake until it's too late. I once heard about an investor who purchased a rental property and opted for a basic homeowner's policy instead of a specialized landlord policy. Everything seemed fine—until a tenant accidentally started a kitchen fire that caused extensive damage. When the investor filed a claim, the insurance company denied it, stating that the property was a rental, not a primary residence, and that the policy didn't cover tenant-caused damage.

This costly mistake forced the investor to cover repairs out of pocket, wiping out years of profits. A knowledgeable insurance agent who specializes in investment properties would have ensured that the right policy was in place, covering both the structure and liability protection for tenant-related incidents. The right agent understands the nuances of different property types, whether they are single-family rentals, multiunits, or short-term vacation rentals. They help compare policies across providers and tailor coverage to fit specific investment strategies, ensuring that landlords are never left financially exposed when disaster strikes.

Mentor or Coach

A mentor or coach is an experienced investor who can offer guidance, share lessons from their journey, and help you avoid common mistakes. In my real estate career, I didn't just have one mentor—I had many. When I first started as a real estate agent, I had two mentors who helped me navigate the industry. But when I transitioned into real estate investing, I became what you might call a "seminar junkie," investing thousands into learning from experienced professionals.

I attended two major real estate education programs. One was with Tarek and Christina from *Flip or Flop*, where I paid around $26,000 for their program. The other was Robert Kiyosaki's *Rich Dad* education, which also cost about the same. Beyond structured programs, I followed experienced investors on YouTube, made connections with real estate professionals, and attended REI (Real Estate Investment) groups in California. I actively sought out people who were already successful in the business, learning from their experiences and mistakes. Looking back, I realize that having access to multiple mentors fast-tracked my success and helped me avoid costly missteps that could have slowed me down.

Finding a great mentor isn't always about paying for expensive coaching. You can join local real estate clubs, engage in online forums, and attend seminars or networking events to connect with experienced investors. Many successful investors are open to mentorship if you show initiative and a willingness to learn. Sometimes, offering to assist an experienced investor—whether by helping with deals, analyzing properties, or just being a reliable resource—can open doors to mentorship opportunities that are worth far more than any course or program.

Building a Strong Real Estate Team: The Key to Long-Term Success

Building a strong real estate team requires intentional effort and strategic networking. Consistently attending real estate meetups, webinars, and conferences allows you to connect with professionals and investors who can help grow your business. Asking for referrals is one of the most effective ways to find reliable team members since trusted recommendations often lead to long-term partnerships. However, simply finding someone isn't enough; you also need to vet them thoroughly. Interview potential team members, check their references, and ensure that they understand your investment goals. Clear communication is also essential. Setting expectations early, establishing regular check-ins, and providing feedback helps maintain efficiency and alignment. Most importantly, focus on building long-term relationships. Treating your team with respect and appreciation fosters loyalty and trust, which ensures consistent support as you scale your investments.

With that said, there are red flags to watch for when assembling your team. Be cautious of contractors who provide vague or incomplete contracts, as this can lead to miscommunication and unexpected costs. A property manager with high tenant turnover may show poor management practices, which can lead to lost rental income and frequent vacancies. Additionally, professionals who are unresponsive or dismissive of your goals can hinder your success rather than support it. Surrounding yourself with the right people means recognizing when someone isn't the right fit.

Real-Life Example:

When I acquired my first rental property, I underestimated the importance of having a solid team. I initially tried to do everything myself, from screening tenants to fixing plumbing issues. The stress and workload were overwhelming, and I quickly realized that I was spread too thin. It wasn't until I hired a property manager, connected with a reliable maintenance person, and worked with a CPA that I truly saw my business thrive. The property manager saved me countless hours by handling tenant concerns and maintenance issues, while the CPA's tax strategies alone saved me thousands of dollars in deductions. Having the right team didn't just make my life easier, but it also made my business more profitable.

If you're just building your team, begin by making a list of the key professionals you need. Take the first step by attending a local real estate meetup or networking event this month to form connections. Once you identify potential team members, schedule interviews with at least two professionals for each role. Investing time in finding the right people early on will save you from costly mistakes and set you up for long-term success.

Key Takeaways

Building your team is one of the most important steps in your real estate investing journey. By surrounding yourself with knowledgeable, trustworthy professionals, you will not only reduce stress, but you will also set yourself up for long-term success.

As you grow your portfolio, remember that your team is your greatest asset. Treat team members well, and they'll help you achieve your real estate dreams. Start today by assembling your dream team, and watch your investment goals turn into reality.

CHAPTER 11: FINDING DEALS AND ACQUISITION STRATEGIES

The real estate market is full of opportunities, but the ability to consistently find profitable deals is what separates successful investors from those who struggle. Whether you're new to real estate or looking to sharpen your skills, this chapter will cover the art and science of finding great deals and the strategies to acquire them effectively.

Why Finding Good Deals Matters

In real estate, your profit isn't just in the sale; it is often locked in the moment you make the purchase. A well-negotiated deal can mean the difference between a rewarding investment and a costly mistake. That's why experienced investors swear by the saying, "You make money when you buy." Finding a great deal isn't just about getting a discount, but it's about laying the foundation for success in every aspect of your investment.

For starters, securing a great deal supercharges your cash flow. When you buy at a lower price, your monthly returns are higher, giving you more income to save, reinvest, or grow your portfolio. Think of cash flow as the fuel that keeps your real estate engine running. A good deal ensures that you're filling up with premium from day one.

A strong deal also helps you build equity fast. When you buy below market value, you create instant equity—your financial head start. Unlike appreciation, which takes time and the right market conditions, a good deal puts equity in your pocket immediately, ready to fuel future investments or build long-term wealth. It's like taking the express lane to financial freedom.

And let's not forget about risk. A good deal cushions you against the unexpected. Whether it's a surprise repair bill, a market dip, or higher-than-anticipated expenses, buying at the right price gives you breathing room to handle challenges that might otherwise derail your investment. A good deal is your safety net in an unpredictable world.

Ultimately, finding good deals isn't just about the numbers. It's about creating opportunities to grow your wealth, protect your investments, and secure your financial future. By mastering the art of finding great deals, you'll not only stand out as a smart investor, but you will also pave the way for lasting success in real estate.

Sources for Finding Real Estate Deals

One of the biggest secrets in real estate isn't about how much money you have or how perfect your credit score is; it's about how good you are at finding deals. Think of it like searching for hidden treasure. The investors who consistently win aren't always the ones with the deepest pockets; they're the ones who know exactly where to look. Whether you are a new investor or an experienced one with several properties, finding all the places where deals are available gives you an unfair advantage. Some of these deals are out in the open for everyone to see—and others? Well, they're tucked away, waiting for the sharp-eyed investor to grab them. Let's dive into some of the best sources to find your next real estate gem.

MLS (Multiple Listing Service)

The MLS is the go-to tool for finding properties. It is widely used by buyers, sellers, and real estate agents. While competition for properties listed on the MLS is fierce, a savvy real estate agent who can identify undervalued properties gives you a significant edge. Some investors argue that the MLS is no longer a good source for finding good deals, but the accuracy of this perception often depends on the business cycle.

For example, during market downturns, such as the period following the Great Financial Crisis (GFC) from 2008 to 2012, the MLS was a gold mine for deals. Property values were significantly depressed, and buyers didn't need to attend foreclosure auctions to snag bargains. Even at auctions, bidding would often drive prices up to match those on the MLS, which reflected the depressed market. In 2012, as the market hit rock bottom, deals on the MLS were abundant.

Fast forward to 2025. Many homes purchased during that 2008–2012 window have appreciated significantly. This shows the importance of understanding market cycles and using tools such as the Case-Shiller Index to identify prime buying opportunities when market conditions align. The MLS remains a powerful resource when leveraged strategically in the right phase of the cycle.

Off-Market Properties

Off-market properties are like secret doors in the real estate world. Only a few people know they're there, and those who do often find themselves miles ahead of the competition. Why are they so valuable? It's simple. Less competition means more negotiating power. When a property isn't listed publicly, there's no bidding war driving up the price. You're not fighting against dozens of other buyers, but you're having a quiet one-on-one conversation with the seller—and that opens the door to creative deal structures, better pricing, and terms that actually work in your favor.

Investors love off-market deals because they give flexibility. You're not stuck playing by the rules of the seller's agent or racing against the clock before another offer comes in. Plus, many off-market sellers are motivated. Whether they're dealing with life changes, financial stress, or just want to avoid the hassle of listing, they're often ready to sell quickly and quietly. For savvy investors, this isn't just about buying a property, but it's about creating a win-win deal in which everyone walks away happy, and you walk away with equity and cash-flow potential that others never even saw coming. Here is a personal example:

I have a friend whom I've known for years, and every time we would chat, I would casually mention, "Hey, I'm always looking to buy if you hear of anyone selling." I never pushed, but just kept planting the seed. One day he told me he was ready to upgrade to a bigger home and needed to sell his current one—his primary residence. The best part was that the home he was leaving behind was a classic starter home, exactly the kind of property that makes a perfect rental. He didn't want to involve real estate agents, commissions, or the hassle of showings. Because I'd made it clear that I was a buyer, he offered me the chance to make a deal directly—no competition, no bidding wars. I drafted the contract, worked out a fair agreement, and secured a solid rental property before it ever hit the public market. That's the beauty of off-market deals—they reward relationships and readiness.

Foreclosures and Auctions

Foreclosed properties and auction sales are where sharp investors can score deals far below market value. These properties often come with motivated sellers; the banks or lenders just want their money back and are willing to let go of the property at a discount. That's why auctions and foreclosures can feel like walking into a clearance sale for real estate. The potential upside? Instant equity and higher profit margins, whether you're flipping or holding long-term.

But there's a catch—and it's a big one. Buying distressed properties means stepping into the unknown. You might not get a chance to inspect the property beforehand. There could be hidden repairs, unpaid taxes, or even legal complications attached. That's why seasoned investors always proceed with caution—doing their homework, checking title records, and setting strict budget limits to avoid overbidding in the heat of the moment.

Take Brittany, for example. She was just a few deals into her real estate journey when she spotted a foreclosed duplex at auction. The price was unbeatable—almost half of what similar properties were going for in the area. Excited, she jumped in and won the bid. But once the dust settled, she discovered that the property had severe foundation issues and a hefty bill in unpaid property taxes. It wasn't a total loss. Brittany rolled up her sleeves, negotiated repair costs smartly, and eventually turned a decent profit. But she'll be the first to tell you that the key lesson she learned was to never underestimate the "fine print" that comes with distressed properties.

Foreclosures can absolutely be a gold mine—but only if you keep your eyes wide open, plan ahead, and approach every deal with the mindset of a detective rather than just as a bargain hunter.

Wholesalers

Working with wholesalers can be one of the fastest ways to get access to discounted properties—especially those that might never show up on the MLS. They specialize in finding motivated sellers, securing properties below market value, and then assigning those deals to investors like you for a fee. For busy investors, working with a reliable wholesaler can feel like having a deal-finding machine working in the background, constantly bringing leads to your doorstep.

The real value of wholesalers lies in the time and effort they save. They're often experts at marketing to distressed sellers, negotiating under pressure, and unearthing off-market gems—things that can take significant resources if you're trying to do it all yourself. A good relationship with a trustworthy wholesaler means access to deals without the heavy lifting.

But—and this is key—you should never rely solely on their word.

Even the best wholesalers may not have done a full inspection or accurate comps. That's why your due diligence is nonnegotiable. Always double-check the property's condition, title, and financials before committing.

> *Take Marcus, for example—a seasoned investor in Atlanta. Early on, he connected with a local wholesaler who regularly brought him deals. One day the wholesaler presented a duplex at a tempting price. Instead of jumping in immediately, Marcus reviewed the title, pulled his own comps, and inspected the property himself. He discovered an outstanding lien and a zoning issue that could've made the deal a headache. Because he stayed sharp, he negotiated the price down even further to account for the risk— and ended up turning the property into a solid cash-flowing rental. His wholesaler still earned his fee, but Marcus controlled the outcome by verifying every detail himself.*

Wholesalers can be an excellent tool in your arsenal. Build relationships with reputable ones, but always remember: the best investors trust—but verify.

Online Platforms

Online platforms like Zillow, Redfin, and niche real estate investment websites are like digital gold mines for finding potential deals. These platforms put a world of opportunities at your fingertips, from single-family homes to rental properties and even foreclosures. With just a few clicks, you can uncover properties that fit your investment criteria, often with detailed data such as price trends, property history, and market comparisons. Some platforms even specialize in distressed properties, giving you a head start on finding foreclosures or undervalued homes. Think of these tools as your personal scouting team, helping you sift through the market to spot the diamonds in the rough. The best part is that you can do it all from the comfort of your couch, making the search for your next big deal easier, faster, and more exciting than ever.

Word of Mouth

Some of the best real estate deals don't come from fancy marketing campaigns or hours spent scrolling through listings—they come from simple conversations. Word travels fast when people know you're an investor, and you'd be surprised how often a casual mention can spark a lead. Friends, family members, coworkers, and even the guy at your local coffee shop might have a connection to someone looking to sell quickly and quietly.

One investor I know shared how a random conversation at a family barbecue turned into a gold mine. His cousin's friend had just inherited a property he didn't want to deal with. He had no desire to fix it up, and had no patience for agents or open houses. Because he mentioned he was in real estate, the family connected them. One week later, they had a deal locked down with no competition and no listing fees.

Word of mouth works because it's personal and trusted, and it often uncovers opportunities before anyone else even knows they're available. Keep letting people know what you do; you never know where the next deal might come from.

Tax Deeds and Tax Liens

Tax deeds and tax liens are some of the most overlooked yet most powerful ways to scoop up real estate deals below market value. The idea is simple: when property owners fall behind on their taxes, the government steps in—not to take over the property for themselves, but to recover what's owed. And that's where opportunity knocks for savvy investors.

With tax deed sales, the government actually auctions off the entire property to cover the unpaid taxes. These auctions can be gold mines—you might walk away owning a house for a fraction of its market price. But here's the catch: you're buying the property "as is." There's no inspection period and no guarantees. Some investors have picked up properties that turned into massive wins, but others discovered too late that they inherited a crumbling foundation or a legal headache.

I once heard about an investor named Carlos who snagged a small single-family home at a county tax deed auction for pennies on the dollar. It was rough—overgrown yard, boarded-up windows—but structurally sound. After some sweat equity and smart budgeting, he turned it into a profitable rental within six months. But Carlos didn't just get lucky; he did his homework beforehand, checked for any hidden liens, and even drove by the property to assess the risk.

Tax liens, on the other hand, offer a different angle. Instead of buying the property outright, you're purchasing the debt—the lien itself. The property owners still have time to pay off their back taxes, but until they do, you earn interest on the lien. And if they fail to settle the debt, you may have the right to foreclose and claim the property. It's a patient investor's strategy—less hands-on at first, but potentially just as rewarding.

One investor I knew specialized in tax liens. She treated it like planting seeds—buying up liens in bulk, earning steady interest as owners paid up. Every now and then, one or two properties would slip through the cracks, and she'd foreclose, gaining ownership at a fraction of the price. It wasn't flashy, but over the years, it quietly built her a portfolio most investors would envy.

Both tax deeds and tax liens come with incredible upside, but they're not for the careless. Success here requires thorough research, understanding local laws, and, most importantly, knowing the risks. But for those willing to learn the game, these strategies can open doors to deals most investors never even see.

Evaluating Potential Deals

Finding a property is only half the battle; the real magic happens when you know how to evaluate if it's actually a good deal. Successful investors don't just buy on gut feeling; they run the numbers and make sure the deal stacks up. One of the first things to look at is the After Repair Value (ARV)—what the property will be worth after any needed renovations. From there, you'll want to estimate your repair costs carefully, making sure you're not underestimating hidden issues. Next comes the purchase price—it has to be low enough to leave you with a comfortable profit margin after all is said and done. If you're planning to rent it out, calculating your cash flow is key. What will you actually pocket each month after expenses like mortgage, taxes, insurance, and maintenance? And don't forget to check the property's cap rate, a simple percentage that tells you how strong its income potential is compared to its price. The better you are at crunching these numbers up front, the fewer headaches you'll have down the road—and the more profitable your deals will be.

Acquisition Strategies

When it comes to acquiring real estate, there's no one-size-fits-all approach. Successful investors know how to use different strategies depending on the deal. The most common route is traditional financing, in which you secure a mortgage through a bank or credit union. This works great for properties in solid condition, especially if you're planning a long-term buy-and-hold investment. But when speed is essential, many investors turn to hard-money loans. Yes, the interest rates are higher, but the fast approvals and short-term nature make them perfect for quick fix-and-flip projects. Then there's the world of creative financing, which really separates the average investor from the savvy ones. Techniques like seller financing—where the seller becomes the lender and offers flexible terms—can help you acquire properties without the typical bank red tape. Some use lease options, renting the property with the right to buy later, essentially locking in today's price while building toward ownership. Others employ subject-to deals, in which you take over the seller's existing mortgage, keeping it in their name while you control the property. Don't overlook partnerships either; teaming up with another investor allows you to pool resources, share risks, and divide profits. Just make sure everyone's roles and expectations are crystal clear. And of course, cash purchases are the cleanest, fastest way to close a deal. Sellers love cash offers, and you can often negotiate a better price—but it requires significant up-front capital. The beauty of real estate is that there's more than one way to buy a property; you just have to pick the strategy that best fits the deal and your goals.

Negotiating the Best Deal

Negotiating a great real estate deal isn't about being the loudest person at the table. It's about being the smartest, most prepared person in the room. The key is knowing the market inside and out. When you've done your homework and have researched comparable sales, you know exactly what the property is worth—and you won't get swayed by inflated asking prices. Equally important is understanding the seller's motivation. Are they relocating? Facing financial pressure? Divorcing? A motivated seller is often more open to flexible terms or lower offers. When it's time to make your move, start with an offer that's low but fair; it should leave room for negotiation without offending the seller. And always highlight your strengths: maybe you're a cash buyer, can close quickly, or aren't tied up with contingencies. Sellers love buyers who make their lives easier. But perhaps the most powerful tool in your negotiation toolbox is your ability to walk away. The moment you become emotionally attached to a deal, you lose leverage. Stay calm, stay sharp, and remember that sometimes the best deal is the one you didn't take.

Common Pitfalls and How to Avoid Them

Even the most seasoned investors can fall into traps if they're not careful, but knowing the common mistakes up front can save you thousands. One of the biggest pitfalls is overpaying for a property. It's easy to get caught up in the excitement of a bidding war or the fear of missing out. But smart investors always stick to their numbers, no matter how tempting the deal feels. Another danger zone is underestimating repair costs. What looks like a simple cosmetic fix can quickly turn into a money pit if you're not thorough. Always get multiple quotes, and build in a buffer for unexpected surprises; it's better to overestimate than to watch your profits vanish.

Then there's the mistake of ignoring market trends. Buying in the wrong area or during a market downturn can leave you stuck holding a property longer than planned. Stay plugged in to your local market, watch for shifts in demand, and adjust your strategy accordingly. And perhaps the easiest yet most dangerous shortcut is skipping due diligence. Never assume that a property is problem-free. Thorough inspections, title checks, and research into any liens or legal issues should be nonnegotiable. Cutting corners in any of these areas might save time today, but it almost always costs more tomorrow.

Key Takeaways

Finding great real estate deals isn't about luck; it's about strategy, preparation, and persistence. Whether you're sourcing deals from the MLS, auctions, off-market properties, or through word of mouth, the investor who knows where to look—and how to look—will always stay ahead of the competition. But finding a deal is only half the battle. Knowing how to evaluate, acquire, and negotiate effectively is what turns a good opportunity into a profitable investment. Stay sharp: run your numbers, do your due diligence, and never underestimate the value of understanding the seller's motivation. There's no shortcut to success, but by mastering these strategies and avoiding common pitfalls, you'll build a portfolio that thrives—deal after deal.

CHAPTER 12: MANAGING YOUR SINGLE-FAMILY RENTAL PROPERTY

Exceptional property management is the key to success in real estate investing.

— KEN MCELROY

Owning a single-family rental property is only half the battle; managing it effectively is where the real work begins. Good property management ensures steady cash flow, preserves your property's value, and provides a positive experience for your tenants. In this chapter, we'll cover the fundamentals of managing a single-family rental—from finding quality tenants to maintaining the property and handling common challenges.

Why Property Management Matters

Effective property management directly affects your bottom line. It helps you:

- Maximize Cash Flow: Reduce vacancy periods and minimize repair costs.

- Maintain Property Value: Prevent long-term damage by addressing issues early.
- Ensure Legal Compliance: Stay on top of landlord-tenant laws and avoid costly fines.
- Foster Tenant Satisfaction: Keep tenants happy and increase the likelihood of lease renewals, reducing turnover.

Finding and Screening Tenants

Great tenants aren't found by chance; they're chosen by design. The right tenant will pay on time, respect your property, and make your life as a landlord smooth. The wrong one? Missed payments, damages, and endless headaches. That's why mastering the art of tenant screening is your first line of defense—and your greatest asset. It's not just about filling a vacancy; it's about protecting your investment.

Advertising the Property

Listing your property on the right platforms can make all the difference in finding great tenants quickly. Start with popular rental sites such as Zillow, Apartments.com, Facebook Marketplace, or Craigslist. These platforms attract a wide range of renters actively looking for their next home. If you're working with a property-management company, they can list your property on the MLS, which then syndicates your listing to major websites like Zillow, Redfin, and Realtor.com—expanding your property's visibility across the most popular rental platforms. To take it up a notch, consider creating a system to market your property more effectively. This could include setting up a website and landing pages, or even leveraging a strong social media presence to post ads during vacancies. And don't forget the power of presentation! Highlight key features such as your property's location, amenities, and recent upgrades to catch a potential tenant's eye and stand out in a competitive market. It's all about making your property shine while reaching as many people as possible!

Setting Clear Criteria

Setting clear criteria is key to finding the right tenants and avoiding headaches down the road. Start by establishing minimum standards such as credit scores, income requirements, and rental history expectations. Remember, these criteria may vary depending on the property. For example, in more desirable neighborhoods where you can charge premium rent, it's reasonable to set higher income and credit score thresholds. But keep in mind that not every great tenant will have perfect credit; after all, if they did, they might already own a home! To stay on the right side of the law, check your state's regulations on things like deposit limits and other requirements. Transparency is also crucial; clearly communicate your criteria in the listing to attract applicants who are a good fit. By communicating clear expectations up front, you'll save time, reduce stress, and increase your chances of finding tenants who are reliable and responsible.

Conducting Background Checks

- Verify income through pay stubs or tax returns.
- Run credit and criminal background checks.
- Contact previous landlords for rental history.

I'll never forget a landlord I met named Maria. She owned a beautiful single-family home in a quiet suburban neighborhood: newly renovated, fresh paint, sparkling appliances—the works. In a hurry to fill the vacancy, she skipped setting clear criteria and rented to the first applicants who seemed "nice" and had cash in hand. Within months, rent payments became sporadic. Neighbors started complaining about loud parties. When

Maria finally had to evict them, she discovered holes in the walls and thousands of dollars' worth of damages.

Contrast that with another landlord, Kevin, who took the extra time up front. He had a checklist: minimum credit score, stable job history, clean rental references. He made it crystal clear in his listing and interviews. It took him a couple of weeks longer to lease the property, but three years later, his tenants still pay early every month—and even mow the lawn without being asked.

Maria learned the hard way. Kevin learned the smart way. Both stories prove the same lesson: tenant screening isn't an extra step— it's the step that protects your peace of mind.

Interviewing Applicants

The application process isn't just about forms; it's about reading between the lines and having real conversations with potential tenants. Take the time to ask open-ended questions to get a feel for their reliability and compatibility with your property. Questions like "What do you enjoy most about your current home?" or "What's your typical work schedule like?" can reveal a lot about their habits and how they might treat your property.

Pay attention to red flags such as inconsistent income stories or unexplained gaps in rental history. A friendly chat during the application process can uncover clues you won't find on paper. Are they respectful? Do they seem responsible? Can they afford the rent without stretching themselves too thin? These brief insights— gleaned from tone, attitude, and the way they talk about past landlords—can give you a clearer picture of whether they'll pay on time or treat your property with care.

It's like a sneak peek into their tenant personality—so have that conversation! A good property manager knows the value of a friendly yet thorough interview, and it can make all the difference in choosing tenants who help your investment thrive.

Setting Rent and Lease Terms

Before purchasing your single-family home, research what similar properties in your area rent for. This is called "Fair Market Rent." Use resources like Rentometer.com or MLS, or interview landlords and property managers.

Ensure that the property will provide cash flow on day one when you purchase it. This is crucial to ensure the viability of your investment. Additionally, have a strong conviction that it will continue to cash flow by analyzing market trends, local job growth, and economic stability.

Set competitive rates by comparing similar properties and factoring in unique features or upgrades.

The Lease Agreement

The lease agreement, or lease contract, clearly defines the terms of the rental. In some states, default lease agreements are readily available, and if you live in another country, a lawyer can draft one for you. While downloadable lease contracts exist, none of them will specifically reflect how you want to run your business. Real estate is not just an investment; it's also a business, and you must treat it as such.

You need to establish your own standards, outlining the rules tenants must follow, areas in which you might be lenient, and policies you absolutely must enforce. These standards should also be communicated to your team, including your property manager and real estate agent, to ensure that your business operates smoothly. The lease agreement should clearly specify everything, ensuring compliance with local, state, and federal laws.

Brandon Turner from BiggerPockets once said, "Be fair but firm." If you're overly nice, tenants may take advantage of you. Allowing tenants to pay rent late, for example, sets a precedent and can develop into a bad habit, ultimately leading to evictions. By not enforcing your standards, you're not only compromising your business, but you're also failing to help your tenant. Being overly lenient can contribute to their eviction, which could have been avoided if you had set firm expectations from the start. It's important to enforce standards consistently. By being firm yet fair, you'll foster a professional relationship with your tenants without compromising their ability to stay housed.

Hollywood and mainstream media often portray landlords in a negative light, but in reality, landlords provide a vital service. Government housing projects are often inadequate, and private landlords are filling a gap that governments struggle to address. Take pride in your role as a provider of quality housing. You are serving society and offering something valuable.

You don't have to let niceness jeopardize your business or your tenants' well-being. Stand firm, uphold your standards, and focus on serving your tenants effectively.

I once spoke to a landlord named Steve who owned three single-family rentals in a quiet neighborhood. Steve was a kind guy—he believed in giving people second chances and wanted to be the "good landlord." When one of his tenants, Rachel, called saying she'd be a few days late on rent, Steve shrugged it off. "No worries; just catch up when you can," he told her. His lease agreement technically had late fees and strict payment terms, but Steve treated those policies more like loose guidelines rather than hard rules. And whether he realized it or not, he subconsciously communicated that wishy-washy attitude toward Rachel.

The next month, she was late again. Then the month after that. Steve kept trying to be understanding, letting things slide, but what he didn't see coming was that each time he bent the rules, he trained Rachel to believe that the lease didn't matter and that rent wasn't a priority. Six months later, she stopped paying altogether. It cost Steve thousands in unpaid rent, legal fees, and repairs after the eviction.

Steve later admitted, "I thought I was being nice—but really, I was sending mixed signals." His kindness without boundaries didn't help Rachel; it enabled her to dig herself deeper. That's why treating your lease agreement like the business contract it is—firm, clear, and enforced—protects not only your property, but your tenant's stability too.

On the flip side, there's Lisa—a landlord who made her lease terms crystal clear from day one. One of her tenants tried to pay late once. Lisa politely but firmly reminded them of the policy, applied the late fee without exception, and stood by it. The result? That tenant never paid late again. Lisa didn't lose income, the tenant didn't lose their home, and more importantly, that tenant probably walked away with a habit of prioritizing responsibilities—one they likely applied to other areas of life too. Firm, fair, and no confusion. Everyone wins.

Maintaining the Property

Taking care of your property isn't just about keeping it pretty; it's also about protecting your investment. Think of your rental like a car. If you never change the oil, rotate the tires, or check the engine, you can bet you'll be facing some expensive repairs down the road. Your property is no different.

Good landlords stay ahead of problems. Regular walk-throughs can catch minor issues—such as a leaky faucet or a loose roof shingle—before they snowball into something big and costly. It's smart to have professionals service major systems like the HVAC and water heater at least once a year. A few hundred bucks spent on maintenance now could save you thousands later.

But the real secret is speed. When a tenant reports something broken, jump on it. Fast, reliable repairs show tenants you care, which keeps them happy—and happy tenants are the ones who stick around and treat your property with respect. Having a trusted list of contractors ready for emergencies makes all the difference.

And don't forget the seasons. When winter is around the corner, make sure pipes are insulated and gutters are cleared. In the summer, a quick check on the landscaping and exterior can prevent surprises.

In short, a little attention today keeps your rental profitable tomorrow. It's not just maintenance—it's money protection.

Handling Tenant Relations

One of the most underrated skills in real estate isn't knowing how to fix a leaky pipe or crunch numbers—it's knowing how to communicate. Good communication is the glue that holds the landlord-tenant relationship together. Get it right, and you'll prevent conflicts, misunderstandings, and unnecessary headaches. Get it wrong, and even the best lease agreement won't save you.

Start by making it easy for tenants to reach you. Whether it's a dedicated phone line, email, or even a property-management app, give them a clear, reliable way to report maintenance issues or ask questions. It keeps things professional, organized, and avoids the dreaded "I texted you but never heard back" drama. Plus, digital tools can simplify payment tracking and records, saving you from paper trails and confusion.

However, good communication doesn't mean overstepping boundaries. Respect your tenants' privacy. Always give proper notice before entering the property. Be friendly, yes—but remember, this is a business relationship. Tenants need to know you're approachable, but not a pushover.

And when disputes arise—and they will—don't let emotions get the best of you. Stay calm, stay fair, and refer back to the lease. That document is your anchor. If things escalate, don't be afraid to bring in a mediator or even legal help to keep things professional and by the book. Clear communication and firm boundaries build trust, keep everyone on the same page, and ultimately ensure long-term success for both you and your tenants.

Dealing with Vacancies

Vacancies are the silent killer of cash flow. Every day your property sits empty is a day you're losing money. But the good news? With the right strategy, you can keep downtime to a minimum.

The first step is making sure the property is in top shape the moment your last tenant moves out. No one wants to move into a place with scuffed walls or leaky faucets. A quick, thorough cleaning and handling any needed repairs immediately puts you ahead of the game. And once the place looks spotless, don't settle for amateur photos—high-quality pictures make all the difference in catching a prospective tenant's eye. You're not just renting out a space, but you're selling the idea of a home.

When it comes to marketing, don't just post on one website and call it a day. Cast a wide net; use rental-listing platforms, social media, and even local bulletin boards if you have to. The more eyes you get on your listing, the faster you'll fill the vacancy. And make sure your listing pops. Highlight what makes your property special—whether it's a quiet neighborhood, updated appliances, or a big backyard.

If the market is competitive, sweeten the deal. Offering a move-in special, like a reduced security deposit or the first month rent free, can be the tipping point that gets a qualified tenant to sign on the dotted line.

A well-prepared property, a solid marketing plan, and smart incentives can turn vacancies from a financial drain into a minor speed bump.

Legal and Financial Considerations

Managing rental property isn't just about finding tenants and collecting rent; it's also about running your business by the book. Staying compliant with local regulations and managing your finances efficiently can mean the difference between smooth sailing and a legal or financial disaster.

First, know your landlord-tenant laws like the back of your hand. Every state has rules about security deposits, eviction procedures, and what's required to keep a rental property habitable. Ignorance of the law isn't an excuse, and slipping up can cost you big. Smart landlords keep detailed records—everything from payment history to maintenance requests—so there's a clear paper trail if any disputes arise.

On the financial side, treat your rental like a real business—because it is. Property-management software or simple accounting tools can make tracking rent payments, expenses, and profits easy and organized. And don't throw away those receipts—every dollar you spend on repairs, upgrades, or services could lower your tax bill at year's end.

And if you ever face the tough task of eviction, never cut corners. Follow the legal process to the letter. Serve the proper notices, keep documentation clean, and if needed, consult an attorney. Trying to rush or sidestep the law can land you in court, turning a bad situation into a costly one.

Running a successful rental business isn't just about cash flow; it's also about keeping everything legitimate, buttoned up, and bulletproof.

Pros and Cons of Different Management Options

Managing a single-family rental property isn't one-size-fits-all. The strategy you choose will shape your experience, and each path comes with its own trade-offs.

Some landlords prefer to handle everything themselves. Self-management gives you full control. You decide who moves in, how the property is maintained, and how tenant issues are handled. It's also the most cost-effective option since you're not paying management fees. Plus, direct communication with tenants can foster a strong personal connection. But make no mistake—it's a serious time commitment. Handling repairs, late-night phone calls, and staying on top of landlord-tenant laws can quickly become overwhelming, especially if multiple issues pop up at once. It's not just about saving money; it's about whether you're ready to wear all the hats.

Then there are landlords who enlist the help of a real estate agent. An agent can take a lot off your plate by helping with tenant placement, lease agreements, and marketing the property. You'll still be involved, especially when it comes to maintenance and tenant relations, but the heavy lifting of finding and vetting tenants becomes easier. Of course, convenience comes at a price. Agents charge fees, and their involvement often stops once a tenant is secured, leaving the day-to-day management in your hands.

Finally, there's the full-service property-management company route. This is the true hands-off option. From tenant screening to rent collection to coordinating repairs, they handle it all. Their expertise ensures legal compliance, and their systems keep things running smoothly without you lifting a finger. But with great convenience comes higher costs; management fees typically run 8–12 percent of your monthly rent. And because you're more removed, you'll need to vet the company carefully. If their priorities don't align with yours, you could find yourself out of the loop on crucial decisions.

Choosing the right approach depends on your time, knowledge, stress tolerance, and how involved you want to be. There's no wrong answer—only the strategy that best fits your business and lifestyle.

Key Takeaways

Managing a single-family rental property is not a passive endeavor. It's an active, ongoing responsibility that requires structure, discipline, and intentionality. From the moment you screen a tenant to the day they move out, every decision you make shapes your success.

Effective property management isn't about being overly strict or overly nice; it's about being fair, consistent, and professional. It's about balancing empathy with accountability, communication with clear boundaries, and providing value while protecting your bottom line. Whether you choose to self-manage, hire an agent, or delegate everything to a property manager, the systems and standards you put in place will determine whether your rental becomes a cash-flowing asset or a costly headache.

So take pride in being a landlord. Understand the laws, keep the property in top shape, nurture positive tenant relationships, and always treat your rental like the business it is. When you manage well, you're not just maintaining a property, but you're also building wealth, stability, and long-term success.

CHAPTER 13: ASSET PROTECTION FOR SINGLE-FAMILY HOMES

Real estate is one of the best ways to build wealth, but it's not without risks. From lawsuits to debt and unexpected liabilities, owning property can open the door to financial dangers that could jeopardize everything you've worked hard to achieve. That's why asset protection is so important—it's your shield against potential disasters, giving you peace of mind and security for the future.

Asset protection goes beyond just preparing for the worst. It's about putting a system in place that reduces risks before they ever become a problem. Whether it's protecting your properties from lawsuits, separating your personal finances from business liabilities, or adding layers of privacy to your investments, asset protection is an essential part of being a successful investor.

The risks are real. Picture these: a tenant slips on a wet floor and sues you, a contractor files a claim after a disagreement, or a storm causes major damage your insurance doesn't fully cover. Without proper safeguards, just one incident could lead to a financial disaster. That's why smart investors make asset protection a priority from day one.

It's not a one-size-fits-all solution. Every real estate investor has unique needs, and that's where professionals such as asset protection lawyers or real estate attorneys come in. They can help design a customized strategy for your situation, walking you through options like LLCs, trusts, and corporations to find the best fit for your portfolio.

In this chapter, we'll cover the basics of asset protection and how to use it to your advantage. You'll learn about legal structures, the power of leveraging debt to protect your equity, and common mistakes to avoid. By the end, you'll know exactly how to safeguard your investments and why doing so is one of the smartest moves you can make as a real estate investor.

The Role of Professionals: Why Expert Guidance Is Essential

With asset protection, trying to do it all yourself is one of the biggest mistakes you can make. Sure, it might seem like you're saving money up front, but the risks of getting it wrong can be costly—and even disastrous. That's why working with an asset protection lawyer or real estate attorney is not just a good idea, but it's essential.

These professionals bring expertise that's impossible to replicate without years of training. They understand the details of state laws, tax rules, and the pros and cons of different legal structures. Whether you're deciding between setting up an LLC, creating a trust, or forming a corporation, a skilled lawyer can help you pick the right option and avoid costly missteps.

Take LLCs for example. Setting one up might seem straightforward, but without the right paperwork or structure, you could lose the very protections you're trying to gain. A lawyer ensures that your LLC is properly formed, legally compliant, and tailored to your investment goals. The same goes for trusts and corporations; having an expert in your corner means that your plan will be designed to fit your needs, both now and in the future.

Another big advantage of working with professionals is their ability to keep your strategy up-to-date. Laws and regulations change all the time, and what worked last year might not work today. Your attorney stays ahead of these changes, ensuring that your plan evolves with the times and continues to protect your assets.

Perhaps most importantly, hiring the right professional helps you avoid problems before they start. A well-thought-out asset protection plan doesn't just react to threats, but it stops them before they happen. By putting the right structures in place from the beginning, you're protecting your investments, your financial future, and your peace of mind.

When it comes to protecting what you've worked so hard to build, leaving it to the experts is one of the smartest moves you can make.

Basic Asset Protection Structures: Building Blocks to Safeguard Your Investments

Owning rental properties isn't just about making money; it's also about keeping it. One unexpected lawsuit, accident, or legal mistake can wipe out everything you've worked so hard to build. That's why smart investors don't just focus on cash flow and appreciation—they also focus on protection. Setting up the right legal structures isn't optional; it's your first and strongest line of defense. Each tool—whether it's an LLC, trust, or corporation—is designed to shield your assets and give you control. Knowing how these structures work can mean the difference between growing your wealth safely or leaving it exposed.

LLCs (Limited Liability Companies)

An LLC is one of the most popular tools for real estate investors. It creates a clear separation between your personal assets and your business liabilities, which means that if something goes wrong with a property—like a lawsuit or debt—it doesn't spill over into your personal finances. LLCs are also relatively simple to set up and manage, but the details matter. Each state has its own rules, and proper filing is critical to ensuring that you actually receive the protections an LLC offers. Consulting a professional can help you get it right.

Corporations (S Corps and C Corps)

Corporations are another option for asset protection, though they are not as commonly used by individual real estate investors. They're typically better suited for those with more complex operations or multiple revenue streams. The key difference between an S Corp and a C Corp lies in how they're taxed. S Corps allow profits and losses to pass through to your personal tax return, avoiding double taxation, while C Corps are taxed at the corporate level. Choosing the right one depends on your financial goals and the structure of your investments. A knowledgeable attorney or CPA can help you decide if this route is worth pursuing.

Trusts

Trusts are a versatile and often-overlooked tool for real estate investors. Living trusts and land trusts can provide added privacy and protection for your properties. For example, a land trust can hold the title to a property, keeping your name off public records. This anonymity can make you less of a target for lawsuits. Trusts are also valuable for estate planning, helping you pass on your properties to heirs without going through probate. However, they come with their own set of complexities, so it's important to work with an expert to structure them properly.

Leverage as Asset Protection

It might sound counterintuitive, but borrowing money can actually protect your assets. When you use leverage, such as a mortgage, you reduce the amount of equity in a property, making it a less attractive target for lawsuits. For example, if you owe a significant amount on a property, there is less for someone to take in a legal dispute. This strategy works best when used carefully, balancing the benefits of leverage with the risks of overextending yourself.

By understanding these basic asset protection structures, you can start building a solid foundation to safeguard your investments. Each option has its own strengths, and combining them strategically can offer even greater protection. The key is to tailor your approach to your specific situation and goals, ensuring that your hard-earned assets are secure no matter what challenges come your way.

Key Takeaways

Asset protection is more than just a safety measure; it's also a way to secure the future you're working so hard to build. Whether you're just starting out or managing a growing portfolio, having the right protections in place ensures that your investments, personal assets, and peace of mind are safeguarded.

By understanding the basics of LLCs, trusts, corporations, and even leveraging debt strategically, you can create a strong foundation that minimizes risks. More importantly, consulting with a professional helps you navigate the complexities of asset protection with confidence, knowing that your plan is tailored to your unique needs and goals.

Don't wait until a problem arises to think about asset protection. Start early, consult the experts, and make it an integral part of your real estate strategy. With the right plan in place, you can focus on growing your wealth while knowing you're prepared for whatever challenges may come your way.

CHAPTER 14: EXIT STRATEGIES

A successful real estate investor always has an exit plan. Whether your goal is to cash out, minimize risk, or pivot your portfolio strategy, having a clear exit strategy ensures that your investments stay aligned with your financial objectives. In this chapter, we'll explore the most common exit strategies for single-family rental properties, as well as when to use them and how to execute each one effectively.

Why Do Exit Strategies Matter So Much?

Real estate isn't just about acquiring and managing properties; it's also about having a game plan for how and when you'll eventually move on. A well-thought-out exit strategy gives you the ability to maximize profits by selling at the right time, reduce risk by limiting exposure to market shifts or property-specific issues, and free up capital for fresh opportunities. It also helps you stay flexible, adjusting your investments as your financial situation or personal goals evolve.

Selling the Property

One of the most straightforward exit strategies is simply selling the property. It's clean, simple, and effective; you cash out, take your profits, and move on. I've seen many investors use this strategy when their property has appreciated well beyond what they initially paid, or when they sense the market is peaking and want to lock in their gains before things shift.

Take for example a friend of mine, Marcus, who bought a single-family rental on the outskirts of Austin back in 2014. He got in when prices were still reasonable, the area wasn't fully developed, and he managed to snag a good deal. Fast forward seven years. The neighborhood has exploded—new schools, trendy shops, tech companies moving in. His modest rental doubled in value. Instead of holding on and risking a market correction, Marcus decided it was time to exit. He spruced up the property, brought in a seasoned agent who knew how to position investment properties, and listed it. The result? A bidding war that left him walking away with a healthy profit and a nice chunk of capital ready to roll into his next opportunity.

Selling isn't always about timing the market perfectly, though. Sometimes investors sell because they want to de-risk. Maybe they're over-leveraged, maybe they're tired of the hassles of property management, or maybe life just throws them a curveball and they need liquidity fast. Whatever the reason, a well-executed sale can free up cash and give you options.

The key is being strategic—not desperate. Know the market, position the property well, and treat the sale like the business decision it is.

1031 Exchange

Another powerful exit strategy savvy investors use is the 1031 exchange. On the surface, it sounds like a dry tax code reference—but it's actually one of the best tools out there for growing your portfolio while keeping Uncle Sam at bay. Instead of selling your rental property and handing over a chunk of your profits to the IRS, the 1031 exchange lets you roll those proceeds straight into another "like-kind" property, deferring capital gains taxes in the process.

I knew an investor named Sasha who was the queen of 1031 exchanges. She started out with a small single-family rental in a working-class neighbor-hood. After a few years, the property had appreciated, but instead of cashing out and paying taxes, she set her sights on something bigger. She sold the first rental, quickly identified a duplex in a rapidly growing area, and reinvested her profits—taxes deferred. A few years later, she did it again, trading up to a small apartment complex.

By using the 1031 exchange like a stepping stone, Sasha kept her money compounding and avoided paying capital gains taxes each time. She always worked closely with a qualified intermediary, stuck to the tight deadlines—45 days to identify, 180 days to close—and stayed disciplined about running her numbers.

The beauty of the 1031 exchange isn't just in tax deferral; it's also in the ability to strategically upgrade your portfolio. Maybe you're tired of managing multiple single-family homes and want to consolidate into one larger property. Maybe you're moving from one market to another with better appreciation potential. Whatever the case, it's a tool that keeps your money working harder for you instead of being siphoned off too soon.

Cash-Out Refinancing

Cash-out refinancing is like unlocking the vault hidden inside your property—without ever needing to sell. Unlike a regular refinance, where you might shave a few points off your interest rate, a cash-out refinance lets you pull out a chunk of the equity you've built over time. That's cold, hard cash you can reinvest, use to upgrade the property, pay off high-interest debt, or simply strengthen your financial position—all while keeping ownership of the asset.

One investor I know, Daniel, was a master at this. He bought a fixer-upper rental about ten years ago. He rolled up his sleeves, handled the repairs himself, and patiently rode out the market cycles. Over the years, the property's value climbed steadily. Between appreciation and years of loan pay-down, he built up a solid chunk of equity.

But here's the genius part: Daniel didn't want to sell and lose that steady stream of monthly rental income. Instead, he turned to a cash-out refinance. He lined up a few lenders, compared terms, and secured a new mortgage for more than what he owed—pocketing the difference. That lump sum allowed him to pay off some debts and, more importantly, put a down payment on his next rental property. The kicker? He kept the original property, kept the rent checks rolling in, and now had two investments working for him instead of one.

But why is this strategy so powerful? Because it lets you do something no other strategy can: you can get your initial investment back, unlock your capital gains, and still avoid triggering a taxable event. No capital gains taxes, no selling headaches. You're essentially recycling your equity, multiplying your portfolio, and letting the tenants continue to pay down the new loan.

In short, it's how seasoned investors build wealth: pull your money back out, keep control of your appreciating asset, and use that equity to fuel your next move—all without giving Uncle Sam a dime.

Holding for Long-Term Cash Flow

Some investors play the long game—and there's a powerful reason why. Holding a property indefinitely for long-term cash flow isn't just about collecting rent checks. It's the only strategy that allows you to benefit from all five ways real estate makes you money: cash flow, appreciation, loan pay-down, tax benefits, and inflation hedge—all at once. And the best part? You're not triggering a taxable event like you would when selling.

Take Maria, a landlord I know, who's been doing this for nearly two decades. She started with a handful of single-family rentals in stable neighborhoods, kept them well-maintained, and watched as rents steadily increased. Every month, she collected positive cash flow. Every year, her tenants were paying down her mortgage, building her equity. Property values climbed, adding appreciation. Come tax season, depreciation kept her taxable income lower. And quietly in the background, inflation eroded the real value of her debt while boosting the value of her property.

But here's where long-term holding becomes even more strategic—it's flexible. Whenever Maria built up enough equity, she didn't let it sit there idle. She leveraged it through cash-out refinancing to fund renovations or buy more rentals—all without selling and without paying capital gains taxes. And if she chose, she could eventually pay off a property entirely, enjoying pure cash flow with no loan payments.

It's not a one-size-fits-all approach. You can choose to refinance and grow, or pay down and simplify. The key is that holding long-term lets you play every angle of wealth-building in real estate—without giving the IRS a cut. Your equity compounds quietly, your tenants build your wealth, and you remain in full control of when (or if) you ever cash out.

Lease Option (Rent-to-Own)

A lease option is like offering your tenants the best of both worlds: the chance to rent your property now with the option to buy it later. It's a creative strategy that works particularly well when the market is a bit sluggish and buyers are hesitant to commit—or when you want to keep generating steady rental income while lining up a potential future sale.

I once worked with an investor named Carla who used this strategy brilliantly. She owned a single-family rental in a neighborhood that wasn't exactly flying off the market. The area was solid, but not hot. Instead of lowering her price or letting the property sit vacant, she offered a lease option to prospective tenants: rent now, and lock in the right to buy the property at an agreed-upon price within the next couple of years.

What happened? She attracted tenants who were serious—not just about renting, but about eventually owning a home. They treated the property like it was already theirs, took care of maintenance, and stayed long-term. Carla collected steady rent payments and even charged a non-refundable option fee up front—putting extra cash in her pocket while reducing turnover headaches.

And if they exercised the option to buy? Great! She had a buyer already lined up—no need to list or market the property. If they didn't? No problem. She kept the option fee and continued to benefit from the rental income.

The beauty of a lease option is in the flexibility. You can set favorable terms, retain ownership while collecting cash flow, and offer a path to ownership that appeals to tenants who just need a little time to get their finances in order. It's a win-win that keeps you in control, even when the market isn't cooperating.

Wholesaling

Wholesaling is the art of connecting the dots—and getting paid for it. Instead of buying a property outright, you're selling your rights to the deal itself. It's fast, often low-risk, and can generate profits without ever taking ownership of the property.

I had a buddy, Chris, who made a name for himself in the wholesaling game. He wasn't the guy with deep pockets or a portfolio full of rentals. What he did have was hustle, sharp negotiation skills, and a knack for spotting underpriced properties before anyone else.

One day Chris found a distressed single-family home in a neighborhood ripe for rehabbers. The seller was motivated and the price was well below market value, but Chris didn't want to close on it himself—he wasn't interested in dealing with renovations or tenants. Instead, he locked the property under contract at a great price, then quickly reached out to his network of investors and flippers.

Within a week, he assigned the contract to another investor for a tidy fee, never once pulling out his own capital or stepping foot into escrow. The investor got a great deal on a fix-and-flip project, the seller got their quick sale, and Chris walked away with a paycheck—all without the long-term commitment.

Wholesaling works best when you've got a pulse on your local market, a list of hungry buyers, and an eye for spotting deals others overlook. It's not about holding on to the property or playing the long game; it's about being the middleman, moving quickly, and profiting from the spread.

Passing the Property to Heirs

For investors who think beyond their own lifetime, real estate isn't just a tool for financial freedom—it's a legacy. Passing rental properties down to your heirs allows your wealth to stay in the family, continuing to generate income and offering potential tax advantages like stepped-up basis. Personally, that's always been my endgame. Every rental I buy, my first thought is: *How can I keep this forever?*

With that said, forever isn't always possible.

While I've held on to most of my properties for the long haul, there have been times I've had to make tough calls. Years ago, I owned a rental in a neighborhood that—at first—looked promising, with good tenant demand and solid cash flow. But over time, the area started slipping. Businesses closed and crime crept in, and by the time one of my tenants moved out, it became a struggle just to find new ones. The final straw? People started breaking into the vacant home—not to steal, but to hang out, smoke marijuana, and trash the place. No matter how well I maintained the property, I couldn't renovate my way out of a declining community.

Eventually, I made the decision to sell. Sure, I walked away with an extra $40,000 in profit, but if I'm being honest, I would have much *preferred to keep that property forever, hand it down to my family, and let it keep producing income for generations—without triggering a taxable event. That's always the goal—to build something lasting, something that benefits not just me, but the next generation and beyond.*

If you're thinking the same way, planning to pass your properties down to your heirs, it's critical to have a proper strategy in place. Whether through a trust, a will, or an estate plan, ensure that your properties transition smoothly—preserving wealth, minimizing taxes, and keeping your legacy intact. Real estate isn't just about cash flow today; it's also about creating wealth that stands the test of time.

Factors to Consider When Choosing an Exit Strategy

Choosing the right exit strategy isn't a one-size-fits-all decision. It depends on a mix of moving parts—some within your control, and others dictated by the market. Every investor's situation is unique, but there are a few key factors you should always weigh before making your move.

First, take a hard look at the market conditions. Are you in a seller's market, where demand is high and prices are climbing? Or has the market cooled, favoring buyers and forcing you to be more flexible? Interest rates also play a major role: when they're low, refinancing might make sense; when they're rising, holding long-term or selling at the right moment could be more appealing.

Then there's the unavoidable topic of tax implications. Whether you're facing capital gains taxes, depreciation recapture, or state and local taxes, you need to understand how each exit strategy will impact your bottom line. Some strategies—like cash-out refinancing or passing properties to heirs—allow you to sidestep taxable events altogether, while others may come with a hefty bill if you're not prepared.

Next, think about your financial goals. Are you looking to cash out quickly and free up capital for other ventures, or are you focused on building long-term wealth, letting rental income and appreciation work quietly in the background? Your goals will shape whether you lean toward short-term gains or strategies that support generational wealth.

Finally, assess the performance of the property itself. Is it still producing solid cash flow, or are rising maintenance costs eating into your profits? Sometimes a property that once made sense no longer aligns with your overall plan, and recognizing when it's time to pivot is key.

There's no perfect answer—just the strategy that best matches your circumstances, risk tolerance, and long-term vision. The more intentional you are about evaluating these factors, the more confident you'll be when it's time to pull the trigger.

Key Takeaways

The best investors don't just think about the next deal; they think about the endgame. Your exit strategy is your compass, guiding when and how you turn paper gains into real wealth. Whether you're scaling up, preserving a legacy, or simply positioning yourself for the next opportunity, knowing your exit options keeps you in control. Real estate rewards those who plan ahead—because profits aren't made only at purchase, but also in how skillfully you decide to move on.

CHAPTER 15: SCALING YOUR PORTFOLIO

For real estate investors, the ultimate goal is often to build a portfolio of properties that generate consistent cash flow and long-term wealth. Scaling your portfolio is about leveraging your current investments to acquire more properties, increase income, and grow your net worth. In this chapter, we'll explore the strategies, mindset, and tools necessary to scale your real estate portfolio effectively and sustainably.

The Benefits of Scaling

Scaling your real estate portfolio isn't just about adding more properties; it's also about multiplying your results without multiplying your effort. As you grow, the benefits compound. More properties mean more rental income flowing in every month, providing a stronger, more consistent cash flow. But beyond just boosting income, scaling also allows you to diversify. By spreading your investments across different markets, neighborhoods, or even property types, you reduce your exposure to risks tied to any single location or tenant pool.

Another major advantage is economies of scale. Managing one property might feel time-consuming, but managing ten doesn't require ten times the work—especially when you leverage systems and professional property management. The more units you own, the easier it becomes to spread out costs such as maintenance, repairs, and management fees, ultimately lowering your expenses per property.

Most importantly, scaling accelerates wealth accumulation. Each property you add is another vehicle building equity, generating income, and appreciating over time. It's how you move from simply owning rentals to creating a self-sustaining real estate business that grows while you sleep. You're producing more results for the same amount of time and energy you're already putting in—and that's the power of scaling done right.

The Mindset for Scaling

Before you jump into strategies and tactics, scaling starts with the right mindset. Growing your real estate portfolio isn't something that happens overnight; it requires patience. You're building something long-term, brick by brick, deal by deal. It's easy to get caught up chasing the next big opportunity, but real success comes from staying disciplined, sticking to your investment criteria, and avoiding emotional decisions that could throw you off your plan.

At the same time, adaptability is crucial. Markets shift, tenant demands change, and interest rates fluctuate; you need to be willing to learn, adjust, and pivot when necessary. The investors who scale successfully are the ones who see challenges not as roadblocks, but as opportunities to refine their approach.

And of course, as you grow, risk management becomes more important than ever. It's tempting to get aggressive and over-leverage yourself, but scaling is a balancing act. The goal isn't just to collect properties, but it's also to grow while maintaining financial stability, ensuring that each step forward strengthens your foundation rather than shaking it.

Strategies for Scaling Your Portfolio

Once you've developed the right mindset, the next step is putting that mindset into action with a clear game plan. Scaling isn't about blindly acquiring more properties; it's about being intentional, strategic, and efficient with every move. Whether you're reinvesting profits, leveraging financing, or optimizing systems, each strategy should align with your long-term goals while minimizing unnecessary risks. The key is to grow in a way that's sustainable, in which each property not only adds to your cash flow but strengthens the overall health of your portfolio. Let's break down the most effective ways to make that happen.

Reinvesting Cash Flow

One of the simplest, yet most powerful, ways to scale your portfolio is by reinvesting the profits from your current properties. Rather than pulling cash flow out for personal use, disciplined investors funnel those profits back into the business—saving for down payments on additional properties and using their existing assets to fuel further growth. But here's the key: don't rush to reinvest until your current properties are rock solid. If you don't have sufficient cash reserves set aside for unexpected repairs, vacancies, or emergencies, or if the systems on your existing property aren't running smoothly, expansion can quickly turn into a headache. Your goal should always be to make sure each property operates like a well-oiled machine: self-sufficient, low-maintenance, and stable. Once that's in place, you can confidently use the cash flow to grow, knowing that your foundation is strong.

Leveraging Equity

Another powerful way to scale is by tapping into the equity you've already built in your existing properties. Instead of letting that equity sit idle, you can put it to work—turning one property into the stepping stone for your next. This is often done through strategies like cash-out refinancing, by which you refinance the property at its current, higher value and pull out a portion of that equity as cash. Alternatively, some investors use a Home Equity Line of Credit (HELOC), giving them flexible access to funds based on their property's equity, which they can draw from as needed.

For example, imagine you own a rental worth $300,000 with a $150,000 mortgage balance. If you refinance at 75 percent loan-to-value, you can borrow up to $225,000—giving you $75,000 in cash after paying off the original loan. That's enough for a down payment on another property, or to cover renovations and boost returns. The beauty of this approach is that you're not injecting new capital; you're recycling the wealth you've already built, allowing you to grow without having to start from scratch every time.

Of course, the key is making sure the numbers make sense. Leveraging equity can be a powerful accelerator, but only if your new investments are well-chosen and your existing properties can comfortably support the added debt load.

House Hacking

One of the most accessible strategies for new and seasoned investors alike is house hacking. It's a simple concept but is incredibly effective: live in part of the property while renting out the rest to offset your mortgage and expenses. Many investors get their start this way, building equity faster while keeping their personal living costs low.

Typically, this is done by purchasing a small multiunit property such as a duplex, triplex, or fourplex. You live in one unit and rent out the others, often covering most or even all of your mortgage payment with the rental income. But house hacking isn't limited to multifamily; some investors rent out spare bedrooms or accessory dwelling units (ADUs) in single-family homes, applying the same principle.

The beauty of house hacking is that it accelerates your ability to save for your next property. With your living expenses reduced—or even eliminated—you can stash away more cash while letting the property's appreciation and loan pay-down quietly build your wealth in the background. It's a smart, low-risk way to get into the game and scale up without overextending yourself financially.

Partnering with Other Investors

Sometimes scaling alone can only take you so far. That's where partnerships come in—allowing you to pool resources, share risks, and gain access to deals that might be out of reach on your own. The key to a successful partnership is finding someone who complements your strengths. Maybe you have the capital but not the time to manage properties, while your partner has the operational expertise but lacks funding. By teaming up, you both get to move faster and tackle larger opportunities.

But partnerships aren't something to jump into casually. Clear communication and clear agreements are everything. You need to define each person's role and responsibilities, and how profits (or losses) will be shared. A solid legal agreement up front ensures that everyone is on the same page, minimizing misunderstandings down the road. When done right, partnerships can supercharge your portfolio growth while distributing the workload and reducing personal exposure.

Investing in Different Markets

One of the smartest moves you can make as you scale is to look beyond your own backyard. It's tempting to keep investing close to home; after all, you know the neighborhoods, the trends, and the quirks. But focusing too narrowly on a single market can expose you to unnecessary risk. Imagine if all your properties were concentrated in that one part of Florida hit hard by a hurricane, or if every property you owned was in a Los Angeles neighborhood devastated by wildfires. Entire portfolios have crumbled under the weight of localized disasters or economic downturns. I've seen this firsthand.

I knew an investor—let's call her Jessica—who built a solid portfolio of single-family rentals, all in one mid-sized city in the Midwest. For years, it worked beautifully. The market was stable, cash flow was steady, and Jessica felt confident because everything was close by. But then the local auto plant, the city's biggest employer, shut down. Overnight, rental demand dried up. Vacancies soared. Property values dropped. Suddenly Jessica's entire portfolio—every single property—was under pressure because it was all tied to the fate of that one local economy.

Contrast that with another investor I know—Stephen. He started locally but made a point to diversify as he scaled—adding properties in Texas, Georgia, and even a few out West. When one market slowed, another picked up the slack. Stephen built local teams in each city— including property managers, agents, and contractors—so he didn't need to micromanage. Today, his portfolio is resilient, spread across different markets, and not overly dependent on any single region's economy or weather patterns.

Diversifying geographically isn't just about chasing better deals; it's also about safeguarding your entire portfolio. Research areas with strong job growth, population increases, and sound economic fundamentals. Surround yourself with a reliable local team, and you can confidently grow beyond your zip code while reducing the risk of being blindsided by forces outside of your control.

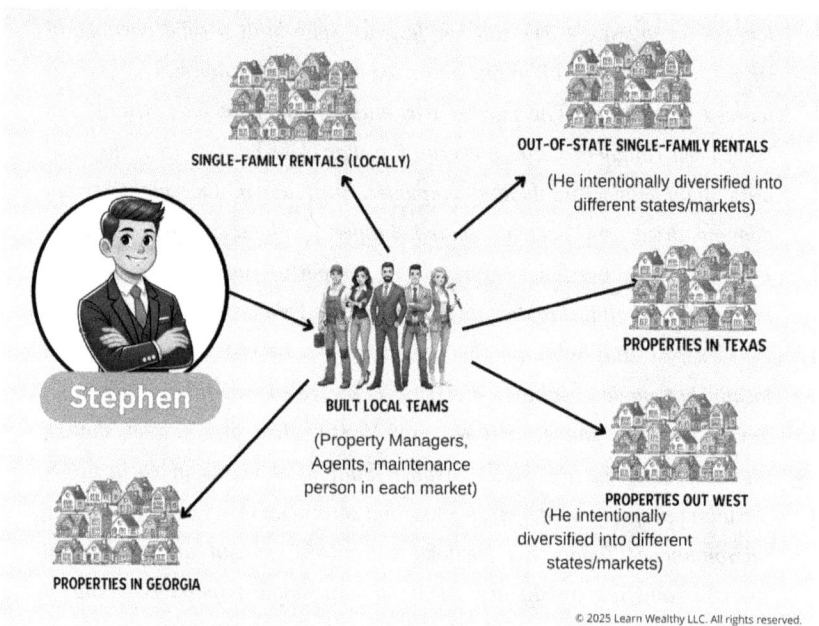

Figure: Stephen's Rental Portfolio Strategy Stephen expanded his single-family rentals by investing both locally and out of state. He built teams in each market to manage his properties passively.

Utilizing Creative Financing

Creative financing isn't just for getting your first deal; it's also one of the smartest ways to scale when traditional financing starts to slow you down. It's about leveraging opportunities that others overlook, especially when capital is tight or when lenders start scrutinizing your growing portfolio a little too closely.

I knew an investor named Caia who mastered this approach. Early in her career, she secured a few properties through conventional loans, but as her portfolio expanded, the banks became less eager to keep lending. Instead of tapping out, she pivoted to creative financing strategies to keep the momentum going.

One of her biggest breakthroughs came when she met a seller who owned several rental properties free and clear but was ready to retire.

Rather than going the usual route, Caia negotiated seller financing—offering favorable terms to the seller in exchange for a lower down payment and manageable monthly payments. That deal alone added three properties to her portfolio without needing to come up with large chunks of cash or jump through hoops with the bank.

Later, she picked up another property through a subject-to deal. The seller was struggling to keep up with payments and just wanted out. Caia took over the mortgage, stepped into an already low interest loan, and added yet another cash-flowing asset to her growing portfolio—all without draining her reserves.

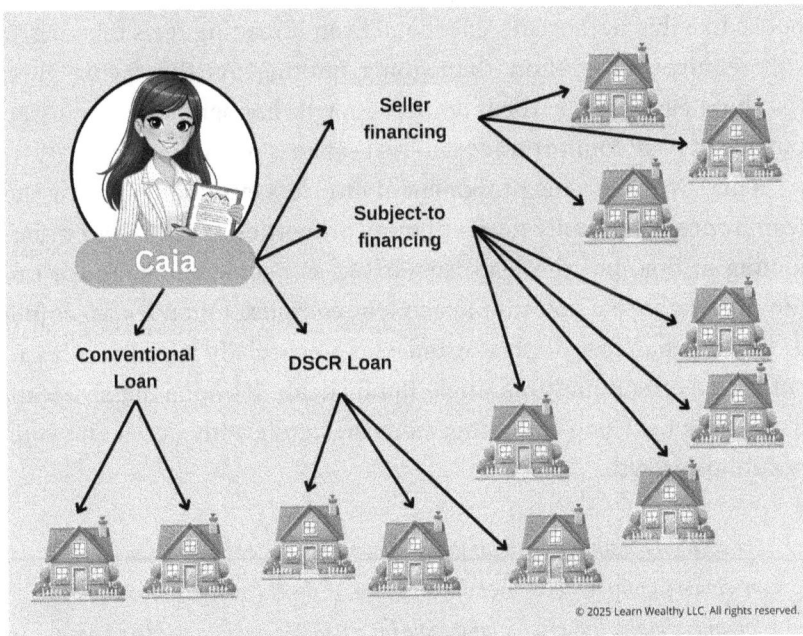

Figure: Caia's Creative Financing Strategy Caia grew her rental portfolio using a mix of financing options—including seller financing, subject-to deals, DSCR loans, and conventional loans—to scale across multiple properties.

By strategically using creative financing, Caia didn't have to pause her growth every time capital ran low or lending guidelines tightened. She scaled faster, structured deals on her terms, and kept her money working—proving that the real magic of creative financing is how it removes the ceiling on how far and how fast you can grow.

Scaling with Multifamily Properties

Single-family homes are fantastic investments. They're a great way to enter the world of real estate. They are easy to acquire, easy to manage, and relatively straightforward to buy and sell. There's also nothing wrong with sticking to them long-term. But here's the thing: easy isn't always what leads to real growth.

We don't go to the gym hoping for an easy time. We don't pick up books like this because it's effortless. Even if reading feels relaxing, it still requires more effort than doing nothing. As the saying goes, "Nothing easy is ever worth doing." Growth happens when you step outside of your comfort zone, and real estate is no different.

That's why I'm a big proponent of investors eventually making the leap from single-family to multifamily properties. It may seem intimidating at first, but the leap isn't as big as people think. You're not jumping right to a 300-unit apartment complex. Often it's as simple as buying your first duplex or fourplex—especially if you've already cut your teeth on multiple single-family deals. It's not a massive leap; it's just the next step—and that step can significantly accelerate your portfolio's growth.

I've seen this firsthand with an investor named Mica. For years, she focused on single-family rentals—solid properties in decent neighborhoods, cash flowing reliably. But after a while, she hit a wall. Managing scattered properties across town, dealing with maintenance calls from multiple locations, and having to hunt for new deals every time she wanted to scale became a grind. She wanted to grow faster, but adding one property at a time felt like treading water.

That's when she bought her first fourplex. Suddenly the game shifted. Instead of four separate roofs, four sets of utilities, and four driveways scattered across different neighborhoods, everything was under one roof. There was now one location and one property manager. And here's where multi-

family really shines when it comes to scaling: the value of the property isn't based on comps or the whims of the local market—it's based on the income it produces.

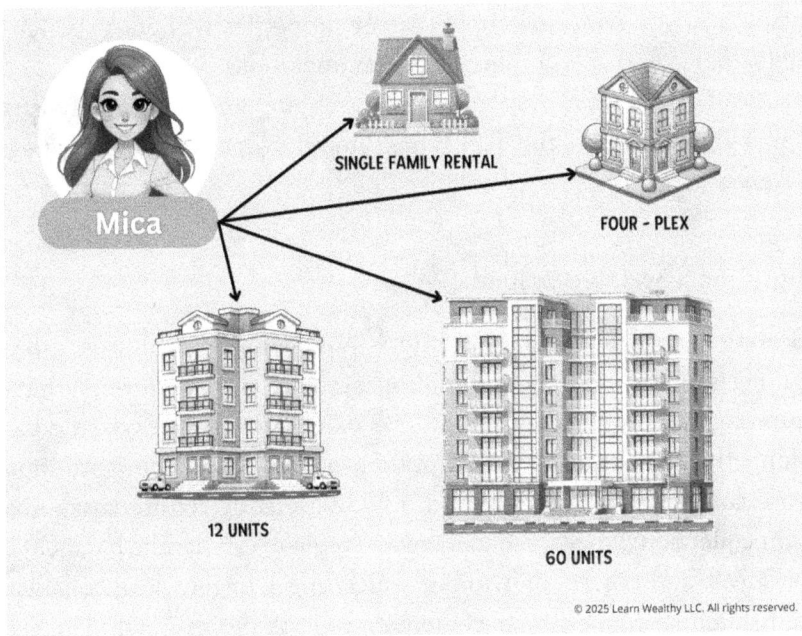

Figure: Mica's Rental Property Progression Mica scaled her portfolio from a single-family rental to a four-plex, then expanded into larger multifamily buildings with 12 and 60 units.

With single-family homes, your property's value is largely tied to what similar homes in the area sell for, regardless of how profitable your rental is. But with multifamily, you're in control. Increase rents, improve operations, and reduce vacancies—and you've directly increased the property's value. Mica realized that managing one well-performing fourplex gave her far more control, stability, and income potential than juggling four separate houses ever did.

She didn't stop there. That one fourplex gave her the confidence, experience, and cash flow to keep scaling, eventually moving into even larger properties. Vacancies in one unit didn't stress her out, because the other units covered the mortgage. Repairs were consolidated. Expenses were easier to manage. Her growth snowballed faster than it ever could have in the single-family space.

The beauty of multifamily is that it's scalable by design. You build bigger streams of income under one roof, you control the value of the asset, and you can move up to larger properties without exponentially increasing the complexity of your operations.

So if you're serious about scaling, stepping into multifamily isn't some giant leap—it's the logical next step that opens up entirely new levels of growth.

Building a Scalable System

Scaling your real estate portfolio isn't just about acquiring more properties; it's also about building systems that keep everything running smoothly as you grow. The more streamlined your operations, the less time you spend putting out fires, and the more time you can focus on expansion. Start by automating routine tasks like rent collection. Property-management software can handle payments, late fees, and reminders without you lifting a finger. Next, consider outsourcing property management entirely. A professional manager can take care of tenant communication, maintenance, and day-to-day issues, freeing you to focus on big-picture strategy. Standardizing your processes is also key. Whether it's tenant screening, maintenance schedules, or lease renewals, having clear checklists and procedures in place reduces errors and saves you from constantly reinventing the wheel. And finally, don't overlook the power of technology. Tools like accounting software, CRMs, and project management platforms keep everything organized, giving you a clear view of your portfolio without getting bogged down in paperwork. The more efficient your system is, the easier it becomes to scale without sacrificing your sanity.

Overcoming Challenges in Scaling

Scaling your portfolio isn't without its hurdles. As you grow, new challenges naturally arise, but with the right mindset and preparation, they're all manageable. Financing often becomes the first obstacle. Traditional lenders can tighten up once they see multiple properties under your name, but that's where working with lenders who specialize in real estate investors—and tapping into alternative financing strategies—can keep deals moving forward.

Property management also becomes more complex as you add units. What was once easy to handle with one or two properties can quickly turn into a full-time job. The key here is building a reliable team—property managers, contractors, handymen—people you trust to keep things running without constant oversight.

Then there's market volatility. Real estate markets shift, interest rates fluctuate, and local economies rise and fall. The best defense is diversification. Spread your investments across different markets and always keep a financial buffer in place so a downturn in one area doesn't derail your entire portfolio.

And finally, be mindful of over-leveraging. It's tempting to grow fast, stacking up debt to acquire more properties. But if your debt-to-equity ratio gets too aggressive, even a small hiccup can ripple into a major problem. Sustainable scaling means keeping leverage at a healthy level—one that supports growth without putting your financial stability at risk.

Key Takeaways

Scaling your real estate portfolio is a rewarding journey that requires strategic planning, disciplined execution, and a willingness to adapt. By leveraging your existing assets, employing creative financing, and building a scalable system, you can achieve exponential growth. Remember, the key to scaling is not just acquiring more properties, but doing so in a way that aligns with your financial goals and long-term vision.

Scaling isn't about how fast you can stack properties; it's about how well you can control, sustain, and multiply them. Done right, you won't just build a portfolio—you'll build freedom.

CHAPTER 16: THE EMOTIONAL SIDE OF REAL ESTATE AND FINAL THOUGHTS

Real estate investing isn't just about numbers, contracts, or properties; it's also a deeply emotional journey. From the excitement of closing your first deal to the stress of managing unexpected repairs, every stage of this process can evoke a wide range of feelings. In this final chapter, we'll explore the emotional side of real estate, how to navigate it, and the mindset you need to achieve long-term success.

The Emotional Roller Coaster of Real Estate

Real estate investing comes with incredible highs: the sense of accomplishment when you close your first deal, the excitement of watching your portfolio grow, and the realization that financial freedom is within reach. There is also a deep satisfaction in providing families with safe, welcoming homes, knowing that you're not just building wealth, but you're also making a positive impact.

But the lows? They're real, too. Unexpected repairs like a leaky roof or faulty plumbing can hit both your wallet and your stress levels. Vacancies and tenant turnovers bring uncertainty, and finding the next tenant can feel like a race against the clock. And then there are market downturns—those periods where property values drop or rental income shrinks due to broader economic shifts—testing your patience and resilience.

Navigating these emotional swings is part of the journey. The key is to expect them, prepare for them, and not let the temporary lows overshadow the long-term rewards.

Managing Stress and Staying Resilient

Building a strong support system is key to success in real estate investing. Surround yourself with other investors who understand the challenges and can offer valuable insights, while leaning on your core team—agents, property managers, and contractors—to help manage the day-to-day load.

At the same time, always keep your long-term goals in focus, whether that's financial freedom, generational wealth, or personal growth. Setbacks will happen; that's part of the journey. What matters is staying committed to your vision and celebrating the small wins along the way. Acquiring a new property, reducing vacancy rates, or completing a successful renovation may seem like an incremental step, but each one adds fuel to your motivation.

Don't underestimate the importance of maintaining a healthy work-life balance, especially if you're hands-on in managing properties. Set boundaries, carve out time for hobbies, family, and self-care, and give yourself space to recharge.

Finally, emotional intelligence is one of the most valuable tools an investor can develop. Self-awareness helps you recognize how stress might influence your decisions. Practicing empathy with tenants, team members, and business partners allows you to resolve conflicts calmly and professionally. It's not just about growing your portfolio, but it's also about growing as a leader.

What Can Real Estate Do for You?

Whether you want to stick with single-family homes, scale into multifamily, or venture into agricultural, industrial, or commercial properties—at the end of the day, this whole investing game is about one thing: what real estate can do for you.

It all starts with your Big Why. Why are you doing this? What's driving you? For me, it's freedom. It's family. It's knowing I don't have to clock in at a job every day. I spent fourteen years working as a registered nurse—a solid, respectable career—but deep down, it wasn't aligned with who I really was. There's nothing wrong with being a nurse. It just wasn't me. I needed something more. I needed control over my time, my income, and my life.

And that's the point I want to hammer home. You are the most important part of your investment strategy. It's not about the house. It's not about the market conditions. It's not even about the broader economy. The real driving force behind your success is you—your goals, your aspirations, and your vision for what this is all supposed to lead to.

Maybe five properties are enough for you. Maybe you want ten. Maybe you dream of owning one hundred doors or growing into larger apartment complexes. Or maybe your calling is to branch into entirely new sectors like commercial or industrial real estate.

Whatever the path, real estate is simply the tool. Your life is the outcome.

Make Real Estate a Fun and Enjoyable Experience

One of the biggest lessons I've learned is that real estate should be fun. It should fit into your life, not the other way around. There are many roles in real estate investing; some you'll naturally enjoy, and others you'll absolutely hate. The key to long-term success is knowing which is which and building your business around that.

For me, Airbnb and short-term rentals were a hard no. Why? Because I realized they required more involvement, more management, and more daily headaches than I ever wanted. I didn't get into real estate to create another job for myself. That's why I've chosen to stick with the simple, reliable buy-and-hold strategy. It gives me all the benefits I want—real estate appreciation (both forced and natural), cash flow, loan pay-down, and tax advantages—without needing to micromanage every detail.

What I love most is how easy it is to delegate the parts I don't enjoy. Property management? Handled. Tenant issues? Outsourced. Honestly, today I'm so removed from the day-to-day operations that even my tenant—who lives right next door—doesn't know I'm his landlord. That's how I like it. It's not fun getting one hundred phone calls a day, and it's not necessary in order to build a successful portfolio.

Even as a real estate agent, I take the same approach. I only work with clients who are eager to learn and respect my expertise. It's not about chasing commissions. I genuinely want to help people, but I'm not desperate. I'd rather focus my time and energy where it's meaningful.

For me, real estate is about business development, portfolio growth, and mentoring. I get excited about developing plans, reviewing deals, and structuring partnerships—not about the minutiae of property maintenance. My business partners feel the same way. When we meet, we're not talking about leaky faucets; we're talking about life, family, and the big picture.

And that's the beauty of real estate, especially single-family rentals: it's incredibly easy to delegate the parts you dislike while keeping full control over your wealth-building strategy.

Ultimately, I've made one clear decision: I only spend my time on the aspects of real estate I enjoy. I delegate everything else to people who are better at it. That's how I've kept my passion for real estate alive. I never want to resent this business, because it's been good to me. So I've built it in a way that keeps me excited, motivated, and free.

Final Thoughts

Real estate isn't just about making money; it's also a personal journey of growth, resilience, and fulfillment. Along the way, you'll face moments that will test your patience, and you will have to make decisions that will shape your future in ways you can't always predict. Persistence, emotional intelligence, and a long-term perspective will bring you both financial success and personal freedom.

Lean on your support network. Delegate what doesn't bring you joy. Stay focused on your bigger goals, and celebrate the small victories—because every step forward is building something lasting. Real estate is a marathon, not a sprint. And with the right mindset, strategy, and passion, there are no limits to what you can achieve.

Thank you for taking this journey with me. Whether you're buying your first rental or scaling an empire, I hope this book has inspired you to keep going and build the future you've always envisioned.

The properties are just tools.

Your freedom is the real asset.

Now go make it your reality.

GLOSSARY OF REAL ESTATE JARGON

A

1. **After Repair Value (ARV):** The estimated market value of a property after all renovations and repairs are complete.

2. **Appreciation:** The increase in the value of a property over time, either through market forces (natural appreciation) or property improvements (forced appreciation).

3. **Asset Protection:** Legal strategies and structures to safeguard investments from risks such as lawsuits or financial liabilities.

C

4. **Cap Rate:** Short for capitalization rate, it measures the return on a real estate investment based on the income the property is expected to generate.

5. **Cash Flow:** The net income from a property after all expenses are deducted from rental income.

6. **Cash-Out Refinancing:** A mortgage refinancing option in which the new loan amount exceeds the

remaining balance on the original loan, allowing the borrower to pocket the difference.

D

7. **Debt Service Coverage Ratio (DSCR):** A ratio used by lenders to evaluate whether or not a property's income is sufficient to cover its debt obligations.

8. **Depreciation:** A tax benefit that allows property owners to deduct the cost of wear and tear on the property over time.

F

9. **Fair Market Rent:** The typical rental price for a property in a given area based on comparable properties.

10. **FHA Loan:** A mortgage insured by the Federal Housing Administration, often used by first-time buyers for its low down payment requirements.

H

11. **Holding Costs:** Expenses incurred while owning a property—including taxes, insurance, and maintenance—especially during vacancies.

L

12. **Land Trust:** A legal entity that holds property titles in order to provide anonymity and protection for the owner.

13. **Leverage:** Using borrowed capital to finance real estate investments, enabling greater purchasing power.

M

14. **Market Cycles:** The recurring phases of growth, stability, decline, and recovery within the real estate market.

15. **Multifamily Properties:** Residential buildings containing more than one housing unit, such as duplexes, triplexes, and apartment complexes.

P

16. **Passive Income:** Earnings generated with minimal effort, such as rental income from properties.

17. **Private Mortgage Insurance (PMI):** A fee required by lenders when a borrower's down payment is less than 20 percent of the property's value.

R

18. **Real Estate Investment Trusts (REITs):** Companies that own or finance income-producing real estate, offering investors a way to earn dividends without directly owning properties.

19. **Return on Investment (ROI):** A measure of the profitability of an investment, calculated as a percentage of the initial cost.

S

20. **Seller Financing:** A financing arrangement in which the seller acts as the lender, allowing the buyer to pay directly over time.

21. **Subject-To Financing:** A method in which the buyer takes over the seller's existing mortgage without formally assuming it.

T

22. **1031 Exchange:** A tax-deferred exchange that allows investors to sell one property and reinvest the proceeds in another "like kind" property without paying immediate capital gains taxes.

23. **Tenant Screening:** The process of evaluating potential tenants based on criteria such as credit history, income, and rental history.

24. **V**

VA Loan: A mortgage option guaranteed by the U.S. Department of Veterans Affairs, offering benefits such as no down payment for eligible veterans and service members.

BIBLIOGRAPHY

- **Biggerpockets.** Various references to real estate investing concepts, strategies, and tools. www.biggerpockets.com
- **Brandon Turner.** *The Book on Rental Property Investing.* BiggerPockets Publishing, 2015.
- **Dave Ramsey.** *The Total Money Makeover.* Thomas Nelson, 2003.
- **Franklin D. Roosevelt.** Quote sourced from public domain speeches.
- **Investopedia.** "70% Rule in House Flipping." www.investopedia.com
- **Mark Twain.** Attributed quote, commonly cited in public domain collections.
- **Robert Kiyosaki and Ken McElroy.** Public video interviews and educational content via Rich Dad YouTube Channel.
- **Thomas Sowell.** *Basic Economics: A Common Sense Guide to the Economy.* Basic Books, 2000.
- **U.S. Department of Housing and Urban Development (HUD).** "FHA Loan Programs." www.hud.gov
- **U.S. Internal Revenue Service.** "Like-Kind Exchanges Under IRC Code Section 1031." www.irs.gov
- **Federal Reserve Bank.** Consumer Price Index Data & Inflation Reports. www.federalreserve.gov
- **National Association of Realtors.** Real Estate Market Data and Trends. www.nar.realtor

🎥 Learn Wealthy on YouTube

Come hang out with me on YouTube — I post free videos every week on:

Come hang out with me on YouTube — I post free videos every week on:

- ✅ Real estate investing strategies
- ✅ Passive income & wealth-building tools
- ✅ Deal walkthroughs & case studies
- ✅ The mindset behind long-term success

🎯 Whether you're a beginner or scaling your portfolio, I got you.

🔗 **Subscribe now:**
YouTube.com/@Learn_Wealthy

🙏 THANK YOU FOR READING!

If this book helped you, inspired you, or gave you a clear path forward, I'd love your support.

If this book helped you, here's how to take the next step:

Leave a review – Help others discover this guide
   https://www.learnwealthy.us/all-my-reviews

Share with a friend – Spread the knowledge

Stay connected:
   ☞ **Learn Wealthy YouTube**
   ☞ **LearnWealthy.us**

ABOUT THE AUTHOR

James Santiago is a real estate investor, entrepreneur, and educator passionate about helping everyday people build wealth through real estate. From managing his own rental properties to developing tools that simplify the investing process, James brings real-world experience to every lesson he shares.

As the founder of **Learn Wealthy**™, he's on a mission to make investing accessible, practical, and profitable for anyone willing to take action.

When he's not breaking down real estate deals or building tools, you can find James spending time with his family, training in martial arts, or creating content to inspire the next generation of investors.

http://www.LearnWealthy.us

facebook.com/LearnWealthyOfficial
x.com/LearnWealthy
instagram.com/learnwealthyofficial
youtube.com/@Learn_Wealthy
tiktok.com/@learnwealthy

For permission requests, contact:

support@learnwealthy.us

LearnWealthy.us

Printed in the United States of America.

First Edition, 2025

ISBN: 979-8-9986854-0-8

✸ Created with Vellum